BOYS

a new play by Ella Hickson

First performance at the HighTide Festival, Halesworth, Suffolk, on 3 May 2012

First performance at The Nuffield Theatre, Southampton, on 16 May 2012

Presented by Headlong at Soho Theatre, London, on 29 May 2012

A HighTide Festival Theatre/Nuffield Theatre, Southampton/ Headlong Production

Production sponsored by Ingenious Media Plc
nd Peter Wilson MBE

INGENIOUS

BOYS

A world premiere by Ella Hickson

A HighTide Festival Theatre / Nuffield Theatre, Southampton /
Headlong Production

MACK	Samuel Edward Cook
BENNY	Danny Kirrane
CAM	Lorn Macdonald
TIMP	Tom Mothersdale
LAURA	Alison O'Donnell
SOPHIE	Eve Ponsonby

Director	Robert Icke
Set and Costume Designer	Chloe Lamford
Lighting Designer	Michael Nabarro
Sound Designer	Tom Mills
Assistant Director	Melanie Spencer
Casting Director	Camilla Evans CDG
Production Manager	Jae Forrester
Stage Manager	Rachael Presdee
Deputy Stage Manager	Kathryn Wilson
Deputy Production Manager	Neil Sowerby
Press Agent for Headlong	Clióna Roberts

The Producers wish to thank:
Elida Trading (www.elidatrading.co.uk) for violin supplies and advice

HighTide Festival Theatre   The Nuffield southampton   **Headlong**

Cast

Samuel Edward Cook (*Mack*)
Sam trained at RADA. Upon his graduation Sam began filming for the popular BBC period drama *Land Girls*, playing the role of Walter Storey. Sam then took the title role of Magwitch in Viola Film's prequel to the Dickens' classic, *Great Expectations*. The film recently had its London premiere and is about to begin its festival tour starting with Cannes Film Festival in May. Sam's credits whilst at RADA include: Heracles in *Heracles*, dir Seb Harcombe, John Proctor in *The Crucible*, dir Toby Frow, The Waster in *Ladybird*, dir Seb Harcombe, Dada in *Our Lady of Sligo*, dir Jonathan Moore, Falstaff in *Henry IV* (Parts 1 & 2), dir Leo Wringer, Bill in *Small Craft Warnings*, dir Alex Clifton, Banquo in *Macbeth*, dir Nona Shepphard and Ferdinand in *The Duchess of Malfi*, dir Helen Strange.

Danny Kirrane (*Benny*)
Theatre credits include: *Romeo and Juliet* (Headlong); *Jerusalem* (Royal Court, West End and Broadway); *The History Boys* (National Theatre); *Tarantula in Petrol Blue* (Aldeburgh Music). Television credits include: *Hustle, Casualty, The Inbetweeners, Doctors, Skins, I Shouldn't Be Alive: Ocean Disaster, Young Unemployed & Lazy, Trinity, The Site*. Danny completed a Physics degree at Leeds in 2007.

Lorn Macdonald (*Cam*)
Theatre credits include: *What We Know* (Traverse); *Six Characters in Search of an Author* (National Theatre of Scotland); *Shine* (King's Theatre); *DNA, The Miracle* (NT Connections); *Parsifal* (Edinburgh International Festival). Film credits include: *Inamórata* (winner of Edinburgh Schools Short Film Festival), *Go: More Than Impulse, Night People*. Television credits include: *Neverland* (Sky Movies); *Mighty Midge* (BBC).

Tom Mothersdale (*Timp*)
Tom trained at Rose Bruford. Theatre credits include: *Romeo and Juliet* (Headlong); *Iphigenia, The Phoenix of Madrid* (Theatre Royal, Bath); *An Ideal Husband* (Vaudeville Theatre); *The Comedy of Errors* (Shakespeare's Globe and UK tour); *A Thousand Stars Explode in the Sky* (Lyric Hammersmith); *Pride and Prejudice* (UK tour).

Alison O'Donnell (*Laura*)
Alison trained at RSAMD. Theatre credits include: *Yerma* (Gate); *The Hard Man* (Festival City Theatres Trust); *My Romantic History* (Bush/Sheffield Crucible); *Eigengrau* (Bush); *Dolls* (National Theatre of Scotland); *Lady Windermere's Fan* (Óran Mór); *The Assassination of Paris Hilton* (Racked/Assembly Rooms); *Mad Funny Just* (Creased); *Phaedre* (Offstage); *Barren, 24 Hour Plays* (Old Vic New Voices); *The Ghost Sonata* (Goat & Monkey); *Broken Road* (Hush Prods); *Love Sex & Cider* (Jacuzzi Theatre); *The Faith Healer* (Hurrah Productions). Television credits include: *Holby City* (BBC); *Feel the Force* (Catherine Bailey Prods); *17 Does It* (Lanarkshire Television).

Eve Ponsonby (*Sophie*)
Eve graduated this year from the Royal Conservatoire of Scotland (formerly RSAMD). Theatre credits include: *The Prince of Denmark* (National Theatre); *The Children's Hour* (West End). Her credits at RCS include *Dracula, The Storm* and *Sweet Bird of Youth*. Eve made her television debut last year in ITV's drama *Above Suspicion: Silent Scream*.

Company

Ella Hickson (Writer)
Ella Hickson burst onto the theatre scene in 2008 with her debut play *Eight*, which won a Fringe First, The Carol Tambor 'Best of Edinburgh' Award and was nominated for an Evening Standard Award. *Eight* went on to tour in New York and at London's Trafalgar Studios and is now regularly performed both here and abroad.

Since *Eight*, *Precious Little Talent* has been performed at Trafalgar Studios, *Soup* at the Traverse Theatre in Edinburgh and *Hot Mess* at Latitude Festival and Arcola tent. Ella has completed a creative writing MA at the University of Edinburgh and spent a year working with the Traverse Theatre as their Emerging Playwright on Attachment. She is a member of the Old Vic New Voices and is currently under commission to Headlong and the RSC. She was the 2011 Pearson Playwright in Residence at the Lyric Hammersmith.

Ella also writes for radio and TV. She is currently in active commission on a number of original drama projects and her first short film, *Hold On Me*, was screened at the London Film Festival 2011.

Robert Icke (Director)
Robert Icke is Associate Director of Headlong. He most recently directed Headlong's production of *Romeo and Juliet* in 2012 and, in 2011, he worked with Rupert Goold in conceiving and developing *Decade* at St Katharine Docks.

Other theatre includes: *Catalysta* (Ovalhouse).

Chloe Lamford (Set and Costume Designer)
Chloe Lamford trained in Theatre Design at Wimbledon School of Art. Chloe's designs for theatre include: *Knives in Hens* (National Theatre of Scotland); *Salt, Root and Roe* (Donmar Warehouse at Trafalgar Studios); *Disco Pigs, Sus* (Young Vic); *The Gate Keeper* (Manchester Royal Exchange); *On The Record* (Arcola); *Rhetoric* (Greyscale at the Almeida); *Ghost Story* written and directed by Mark Ravenhill (Sky Arts Live Drama season); *My Romantic History* (Sheffield Crucible/Bush); *Joseph K, The Kreutzer Sonata* (Gate); *Songs From A Hotel Bedroom* (Linbury Studio ROH/tour); *it felt empty when the heart went at first but it is alright now* (Clean Break, installation at Arcola's Studio K); *Everything Must Go!* (Soho); *This Wide Night* (Soho/tour); *The Mother Ship, How to Tell the Monsters from the Misfits* (Birmingham Rep); *The Country* (Salisbury Playhouse); *Desire Lines, The Snow Queen* (Sherman Cymru); *Blithe Spirit* (Watermill); *Antigone at Hell's Mouth* (Kneehigh Theatre and NYT); *Silence* (Wilton's Music Hall); *Lola* (Trestle Theatre Company); *Small Miracle* (Tricycle/Mercury, Colchester); *The Wild Party* (Rosie Kay Dance Company); *The Shy Gas Man* (Southwark Playhouse). Her designs for opera include: *The Magic Flute* (ETO); *War and Peace* (Scottish Opera/RSAMD); *The Cunning Little Vixen, Orpheus in the Underworld* (Royal College of Music); *La Calisto* (Early Opera Company). Chloe has also designed various music videos and promos, as well as *The Full Monteverdi*, an opera feature film by Polyphonic Films. Chloe won Best Design at the 2007 TMA awards for her design for *Small Miracle* by Neil D'Souza.

Michael Nabarro (Lighting Designer)

Michael is a graduate of the RADA Lighting Design course. Lighting designs include: *The 14th Tale* (Battersea Arts Centre/tour/ National Theatre); *The World's Wife* (Trafalgar Studios/tour); *The Lady from the Sea, An Enemy of the People, The 14th Tale, The Ballad of Crazy Paola, The Blind* (Arcola); *Catalysta* (Ovalhouse); *Simpatico* (Old Red Lion); *Limbo, 1984* (York Theatre Royal); *Thyestes* (Battersea Arts Centre); *Rivers Run Deep, Fight! Fight! Fight!* (Hampstead Theatre Studio); *Gabriel, In the Heart of America, Salome, Duck Hunting, The Girl on the Sofa* (RADA); *The Ash Girl* (Unicorn); *White People & Cocoa* (Theatre503); *Singin' in the Rain, West Side Story, Orpheus in the Underworld* (Cambridge Arts Theatre); *Of Two Days* (Pleasance, London); *Eveline Syndrome* (Dublin Fringe); *The Revenger's Tragedy*, CASA Latin American Theatre Festival (St Andrew's Crypt); *Twelfth Night* (European tour); *Pirates of Penzance* (Minack Theatre); *Fuente Ovejuna, Translations, Cloud Nine, Dancing at Lughnasa, Who's Afraid of Virginia Woolf* (ADC Theatre). Michael graduated from Cambridge University in 2003 and between 2003 and 2006 was manager of the ADC Theatre in Cambridge.

Tom Mills (Sound Designer)

As composer and/or sound designer credits include: *The Way of the World* (Sheffield Crucible); *Benefactors* (Sheffield Studio); *Huis Clos* (Donmar Warehouse at Trafalgar Studios); *Realism and Mongrel Island* (Soho); *Moonlight and Magnolias, Great Expectations* (Watermill); *Clockwork* (HighTide); *Cinderella, Aladdin* (Lyric Hammersmith); *Electra, Wittenberg, Unbroken* (Gate); *A Midsummer Night's Dream, Edward Gant's Amazing Feats Of Loneliness* (Headlong); *Elektra* (Young Vic); *The Eternal Not* (National Theatre); *Othello* (Assembly Rooms, Bath); *Assassins* (Eyebrow Productions). As composer credits include: *The Littlest Quirky* (Theatre Centre); *Dusk Rings A Bell* (Edinburgh/Watford Palace Theatre/HighTide Festival); *The Prince of Denmark*(National Theatre Discover Programme); *Dick Whittington* (also as arranger; Lyric Hammersmith); *Wanderlust* (Royal Court); *Pericles, Macbeth* (Open Air Theatre Regent's Park). He was music associate on *Moscow Live, Lidless* and *Ditch* for the 2010 Hightide Festival. As composer and musical director credits include: *Breathing Irregular* (Gate); *Oliver Twist* (Storm on the Lawn at The Egg, Theatre Royal Bath). As musical director, composer and sound designer credits include: *The Jungle Book, The Grimm Brothers' Circus, Metropolis* (The Egg, Theatre Royal Bath). As musical director: *The Kreutzer Sonata* (Gate); *Return to the Forbidden Planet* (Bath Spa Music Society); *Band of Blues Brothers* (Panthelion Productions).

Melanie Spencer (Assistant Director)

Melanie studied at UEA, RADA and Kings College, London and has just been appointed as Creative Associate at the Gate. As assistant director credits include: *Bea* by Mick Gordon (Soho) and *Wittenberg* by David Davalos (Gate). As director: *Chicken* by Freddie Machin (Southwark Playhouse); *Sense* by Anja Hilling (Hen & Chickens); *Honest* by DC Moore (George on the Strand).

 HighTide Festival Theatre

New Theatre for Adventurous Audiences

'Sharp, irreverent and fresh' *Daily Telegraph*

HighTide Festival Theatre is a national theatre company and engine room for the discovery, development and production of exceptional new playwrights.

Under Artistic Director Steven Atkinson, the annual HighTide Festival in Suffolk has become one of the UK's leading theatre events, and in 2012 we are excited to premiere 18 new works. HighTide's productions then transfer nationally and internationally in partnerships that have included: the Bush Theatre (2008 & 2009), National Theatre (2009), Old Vic Theatre (2010), Ambassador Theatre Group/West End (2011), to the Edinburgh Festival (2008, 2010 & 2011) and internationally to the Australian National Play Festival (2010).

HighTide receives, considers and produces new plays from all around the world, every play is read and the festival is an eclectic mix of theatre across several venues in Halesworth, Suffolk. Our artistic team and Literary Department are proud to develop all the work we produce and we offer bespoke development opportunities for playwrights throughout the year.

HighTide Festival Theatre is a National Portfolio Organisation of Arts Council England.

A Brief History

The Sixth HighTide Festival in 2012

Luke Barnes, Jon Barton, Ollie Birch, Mike Daisey, Joe Douglas, Vickie Donoghue, Tom Eccleshare, Kenny Emson, Berri George, Karis Halsall, Nancy Harris, Ella Hickson, Branden Jacobs-Jenkins, Mona Mansour, Laura Marks, Ian McHugh, Jon McLeod, Shiona Morton Laura Poliakoff, Mahlon Prince, Stella Fawn Ragsdale, Stephanie Street, Philip Wells, Nicola Werenowska, Alexandra Wood

The sixth HighTide Festival in 2012 will premiere eighteen plays in world and European premiere productions in partnerships with emerging companies and leading theatres including: Bad Physics, curious directive, Escalator East to Edinburgh, Headlong, Halesworth Middle School, Latitude Festival, Lucy Jackson, macrobert, nabokov, The Nuffield Southampton, The Public Theater, Soho Theatre, Utter.

Vickie Donoghue's *Mudlarks* will transfer to Theatre503 in a co-production with Lucy Jackson.

Luke Barnes' *Eisteddfod* will transfer to the 2012 Latitude Festival.

Joe Douglas' *Educating Ronnie* will transfer to the 2012 Edinburgh Festival produced in association with macrobert and Utter.

Luke Barnes' *Bottleneck* will premiere at the 2012 Edinburgh Festival.

Charitable Support
HighTide is a registered charity (6326484) and we are grateful to the many organisations and individuals who support our work, including Arts Council England and Suffolk County Council.

Trusts and Foundations
The Bulldog Arts Fund, The Chivers Charitable Trust, The Coutts Charitable Trust, The DC Horn Foundation, The Eranda Foundation, The Ernest Cook Charitable Trust, Esmée Fairbairn Foundation, The Foyle Foundation, The Garrick Charitable Trust, The Genesis Foundation, IdeasTap, Jerwood Charitable Foundation, The Leche Trust, The Mackintosh Foundation, The Peggy Ramsay Foundation, Scarfe Charitable Trust, The Suffolk Foundation, SOLT/Stage One Bursary for New Producers, Harold Hyam Wingate Foundation, subsidised rehearsal space provided by Jerwood Space.

Business Sponsorship
ACTIV, AEM International, Ingenious Media Plc, Lansons Communications, Plain English.

Major Donors
Peter Fincham, Nick Giles, Bill and Stephanie Knight, Clare Parsons and Tony Langham, Tony Mackintosh and Criona Palmer, Albert Scardino, Peter Wilson MBE.

With thanks to all our Friends of the Festival.

The Nuffield Theatre, on the University of Southampton's campus, is one of the South's leading producing theatres, funded by Arts Council England, Southampton City Council, Hampshire County Council and the University of Southampton.

Once a company whose prime activity was the main house production of new plays and 'neglected classics', The Nuffield now operates at many different scales, producing and presenting world-class performances into its theatre and a range of other spaces; commissioning new plays/ productions; developing professional talent; touring; collaborating internationally; and offering a comprehensive range of educational and participatory activities.

Nuffield productions and co-productions often win critical acclaim and awards, whilst the company regularly presents, and collaborates with the best theatre companies and artists from this country and abroad.

The Nuffield has become a vital artistic resource for Southampton, and as well as its core programme, the company is a founding partner in Art and the Heart, Southampton's City animation/audience development project. For *Art at the Heart*, The Nuffield is bringing four extraordinary projects to Southampton this year: *Titanic from Prow to Stern* in April – an installation in the centre of the city as part of the centenary year commemorative programme; in the summer, Generik Vapeur's *Waterlitz* – a giant installation and performance piece that continues our partnership with ZEPA, the European Zone of Artistic Projects; *The Rememberers* with Apples and Snakes at a secret location, and Periplum's *The Art of Demonstration* in autumn.

The Nuffield Theatre plays a strong role in talent development in theatre in the South East region and further afield, including its acclaimed writers' group for aspiring playwrights, several of whom have gone on to win professional acclaim.

As part of talent development, each year The Nuffield co-produces with Headlong Theatre and provides a mentored opportunity to a talented emerging director to work on a major classic. This year's tour of *Romeo and Juliet* was a huge hit with both audiences and critics.

Boys, The Nuffield's first co-production with HighTide Festival Theatre, further expands this work as it is also co-produced by Headlong and directed by Robert Icke, the director of *Romeo and Juliet*. All three companies share a desire to nurture and stage exciting new work and provide opportunities for exceptionally talented individuals – as well as for adventurous audiences to experience the work of some of the best new artists working in the UK.

The Nuffield also nurtures the talents of teachers, pupils and non professionals in the region and we are the southern partners in two projects with the RSC – a learning and participation network for schools , and Open Stages, a project for amateur theatre.

For more information on what's happening at The Nuffield, please visit www.nuffieldtheatre.co.uk, Facebook on.fb.me/Nuffield or Twitter@nuffieldtheatre

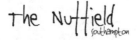

For the Nuffield

❧

Signed and audio described performances and set feels: Thursday 24th May 7.30 p.m.
In accordance with the requirements of the licensing authority, the audience may leave at the end of the performance by all exit doors.
All gangways, corridors, staircases and passageways which afford a means of exit shall be kept entirely free from obstruction.
Persons shall not be permitted to stand or sit in any of the gangways except in positions authorised by the licensing authority and in numbers indicated in the notices exhibited in the those positions.

Headlong

Headlong makes exhilarating, provocative and spectacular
new work to take around the country and around the world.

'*The country's most
exciting touring company*'

Daily Telegraph

'*Rupert Goold is the finest
director of his generation*'

Evening Standard

Headlong is one of the UK's leading theatre companies. Led by award-winning
Artistic Director Rupert Goold, Headlong is dedicated to new ways of making
theatre. We collaborate with the most exciting and adventurous theatre artists
in the country and provide them with the time, resources and creative support
to allow them to make their most challenging work.

We are interested in theatre that asks provocative questions of the world we live
in today in the most vibrant and theatrical forms we can imagine. The focus of
our work is new writing but we also look to develop new and emerging artists
through dynamic and ambitious revivals. We run workshops and placement
programmes for the writers, directors, designers and producers of the future;
practitioners who have emerged under Headlong's support are now some of
the leading theatre artists around the world.

Previous work includes:

Romeo and Juliet (UK tour); *Decade* (St Katharine Docks); *Earthquakes in London*
(National Theatre/UK tour); *ENRON* (Chichester Festival Theatre/Royal Court/West
End/UK tour/Broadway); *Elektra* (Young Vic); *Faustus, Salome* (UK tour/Hampstead
Theatre); *Six Characters in Search of an Author* (Chichester Festival Theatre/West
End/UK tour/Sydney/Perth); *Edward Gant's Amazing Feats of Loneliness* (UK tour/
Soho Theatre); *King Lear* (Liverpool Everyman/Young Vic); *…Sisters, Lulu, Medea
Medea* (The Gate); *The Last Days of Judas Iscariot* (Almeida Theatre); *Rough
Crossings, Angels in America* (UK tour/Lyric, Hammersmith); *A Midsummer Night's
Dream, The English Game, The Winter's Tale, Restoration, Paradise Lost* (UK tour).

Forthcoming shows include:

The Effect by Lucy Prebble, directed by Rupert Goold. **Medea** by Euripides, adapted and directed by Mike Bartlett. **American Psycho**, book by Roberto Aguirre-Sacasa, music and lyrics by Duncan Sheik, based on the novel by Bret Easton Ellis, directed by Rupert Goold. **Chimerica** by Lucy Kirkwood.

For full details go to **www.headlongtheatre.co.uk**

Headlong Theatre is:

Rupert Goold	Artistic Director
Henny Finch	Executive Producer
Jenni Kershaw	Executive Producer (Maternity Cover)
Robert Icke	Associate Director
Julie Renwick	Finance Manager
Lindsey Alvis	Assistant Producer
Ellie Collyer-Bristow	Production Assistant (Stage One Apprentice)
Jamie Lloyd	Associate Artist

Catrin Stewart in *Romeo and Juliet*
Photographer: Tristram Kenton

Supported using public funding by
ARTS COUNCIL ENGLAND

www.headlongtheatre.co.uk

BOYS

Ella Hickson

*For the brilliant young men and women of
Stafford Street and 320 Basement*

Acknowledgements

I would like to thank Rob Icke for his hard work and his unfaltering faith, right from the first draft to the first night, it wouldn't have happened without him. I would like to thank the cast and crew for their ideas, commitment and conviction, it has been a pleasure. My thanks go to Lindsey Alvis and all at Headlong, HighTide, Nuffield and Peter Wilson for their generous support. I am indebted to Jess Cooper, Simon Stephens and all at the Lyric Hammersmith for their continued help and advice.

I would like to thank the inhabitants of Stafford Street, Edinburgh, and 320 Basement, London, for their friendship and for great times spent around the kitchen table.

My thanks to Tim for letting me talk it through, for taking the time to give good advice and for adding to the argument that we don't have to do it alone. Milk.

E.H.
London, 2012

'No man is an iland, intire of it selfe; every man is a peece of the Continent, a part of the maine; if a clod bee washed away by the Sea, Europe is the lesse, as well as if a Promontorie were, as well as if a Mannor of thy friends or of thine owne were; any mans death diminishes me, because I am involved in Mankinde…'

John Donne
Meditation 17: Devotions upon Emergent Occasions

'The crisis of modern society is precisely that the youth no longer feel heroic in the plan for action that their culture has set up. They don't believe it empirically true to the problems of their lives and times.

Ernest Becker
The Denial of Death

6

Characters

BENNY
MACK
TIMP
CAM
LAURA
SOPHIE

A forward slash (/) in the text indicates interrupted speech.

Square brackets [ ] indicate unspoken speech.

This text went to press before the end of rehearsals and so may differ slightly from the play as performed.

ACT ONE

Scene One

The kitchen of a five-man student flat, Edinburgh.

An unusually hot summer.

Rubbish bags pile up in the corners.

There are five chairs; one of these chairs is never touched unless indicated.

The kitchen is thick with the usual debris: tobacco packets, Rizlas, wine bottles and beer cans, dirty washing lies around, ashtrays are overflowing, pizza boxes and kebab boxes are scattered, plates and pots pile up in the sink.

On top of this – this morning – there are remnants of a party the night before: helium balloons populate the ceiling, there are streamers and party hats about, a fake pirate's sword is stuck into the middle of the table, a 'Barclay's' sign is propped up on the side 'We'll loan you the best years of your life'.

CAM sleeps curled beneath the table. He is wearing dinosaur pyjamas and still has a pirate hat on from the night before.

BENNY enters in his dressing gown; he winces against the morning sun, he doesn't see CAM. BENNY collects a bowl, some milk and a spoon. He goes to his cupboard and takes out a packet of Coco Pops, pours himself a bowl – a toy lands in his bowl. BENNY is delighted, he unwraps the toy as if he was a kid – he holds up a tiny toy soldier and then thinks to tell his best friend. An acute sadness falls. BENNY places the little soldier out in front of him on the table and stares at it. He puts the toy in his dressing-gown pocket. BENNY approaches another cupboard – pulls the bin over to it and braces himself. He breathes in deeply – and begins to unpack the cupboard into the bin: jams, mouldy bread, noodle packets, tins of baked beans – he reaches a packet of Coco Pops and looks at it. He takes the soldier from his pocket – puts it into the box of Coco Pops and puts the box on the table. He returns to the cupboard.

BENNY *stands*.

BENNY *takes a balloon – pulls it down and then lets it float back up to the ceiling*.

BENNY *climbs up on top of the fridge and looks out across the kitchen*.

TIMP – *impish and toned, tattooed, pierced and sporting a Mohican – wears a pair of tight pink boxers with 'Spank' written across the arse. He has an eyepatch over one eye. He walks stealthily over to the kettle and begins making two cups of tea, two pieces of toast*.

BENNY. Morning… Captain.

> TIMP *startles slightly, turns and notices* BENNY *on top of the fridge*.

TIMP. Oh 'ello.

BENNY. What happened in here then?

TIMP. What do you mean?

BENNY. The balloons.

TIMP. Party.

BENNY. Oh really. (*Beat*.) Laura here?

TIMP. No – why?

BENNY. Who's the other cup for?

TIMP. Oh – this? Cam.

BENNY. He up?

TIMP. Yeah – rehearsing. What you doing up on the / (*Notices that the cupboard has been opened and is half-cleared out*.)

BENNY. I thought I'd /

TIMP. Should have fucking been here last night, Benny-boy!

BENNY. Funny being up here at this height.

TIMP. Pirate party for the new intake!

BENNY. It's end of term.

TIMP. Prospective students, looking around, open day – fresher than freshers.

BENNY. Feels like you can control everything.

TIMP. Fresh meat, Benny!

BENNY *puts his hands out as if he is conducting the kitchen.*

BENNY. I'm magic, see; I'm making your tea turn into steam.

TIMP. Well, stop it – I'll come and tell ya all about it, one sec.

BENNY *keeps his hands out, trying to move the objects of the room about.*

As TIMP *goes out the door slams behind him. The noise wakes up* CAM *who bangs his head on the bottom of the table.* BENNY *is startled, thinking he has done it.*

CAM. Whathafuareyouwhyisthe.

BENNY. Cam?

CAM *crawls out from under the table, looks woozily around the place.*

CAM. Oh fuck.

BENNY. Aren't you rehearsing?

CAM. Fuck off. What time is it?

BENNY. Elevenish.

CAM. Oh fuck.

TIMP *re-enters holding just one cup of tea and sees* CAM – *a beat whilst* TIMP *creates his story.*

TIMP. There you bloody are.

TIMP *hands* CAM *the cup of tea.*

CAM (*befuddled*). Cheers.

BENNY. Where's yours?

TIMP. What?

BENNY. Tea?

CAM. You want this?

TIMP. Drank it.

BENNY. But you were –

CAM. Don't fancy it; too hot.

CAM *hands* BENNY *the tea.*

Why you on the /

BENNY (*takes the tea*). Thanks.

CAM. Anyone got any idea what I did with my /

TIMP. You seen the kiddiewink this morning?

CAM. What?

TIMP. The old ankle-biter.

CAM. No.

CAM *sees that the cupboard is open and that it has been half unpacked, he stops in his tracks.*

Oh.

CAM *stops and looks at the cupboard.*

BENNY. I thought I'd /

TIMP. I regret to inform you, Benny-boy, that you may have missed what was almost certainly the best party of the year last night.

BENNY. Again. What time is the concert, Cam?

CAM. Later.

TIMP. You're right – now I think about it all the very great parties happen when you are very not being there and it is deeply suspicious.

BENNY. You alright?

TIMP. Yeah.

CAM *pulls his violin out from under a pile of rubbish – a smiley face has been drawn on it in squirty cream.*

CAM. Oh, for fuck's sake.

TIMP. Oh dear.

CAM. Most important concert of my life and I'm going to smell like a fucking yogurt.

BENNY. What is wrong with you?

TIMP. Why nothing, kind sir, could I interest you in a beverage?

CAM. Are you…? Oh – yeah – right.

BENNY. What?

CAM. I was meant to remind you that you put your E in your aspirin bottle last night.

TIMP. Did I?

CAM. One of the girl's rape alarms went off; you thought it was the police – you put all your drugs into your painkillers.

TIMP. Oh fuck – I'm high.

BENNY. You didn't notice?

TIMP. Yep – yep – now I come to think of it – yep that is what this feeling is.

TIMP *clips* CAM *round the ear.*

CAM. Ow.

TIMP. Course I fucking know I'm high, you mutant ninja retard; couldn't be arsed with a hangover – that's all – besides I'm highly entertaining when I'm highly high. (*Searches around on the table and picks up two more tablets.*) Anyone else?

CAM *goes to take one.*

BENNY. Cam?

CAM. What?

BENNY. You're playing violin in front of three thousand people and a fuck-ton of TV cameras in about five hours.

CAM *thinks about it for a minute.*

TIMP. Oh, come on – that's a TV show I'd watch.

BENNY. Cam? That's your whole career – don't be a dick. What are you doing?

CAM. I'm dead tired of being nervous.

TIMP. Sort you right out, that will.

BENNY. Timp – shut up!

TIMP. Come on – it'll calm him down.

CAM. I really want to.

TIMP. I want a party pal.

CAM. Haven't you got to go to work?

TIMP. You can come – you can practise – we'll have you instead of the radio. Doesn't that sound lovely?

BENNY. Timp?

TIMP. What? Why are you crawling inside your own arse?

BENNY. He's on the front page of the newspaper – he's meant to make fucking history this evening – not dribble on himself with a full fucking orchestra behind him.

CAM. Imagine – not caring, aw just for a second – just imagine…

BENNY. I can't watch this.

BENNY turns to go.

CAM puts the pill in his pocket.

TIMP. You fucking mentalist – you joker – I can't believe you just did that!

BENNY turns back and goes ape-shit.

BENNY. What? What the fuck – tell me you didn't just – spit it out – spit it out –

BENNY launches himself at CAM and starts trying to get his fingers in his mouth before attempting an approximation of the Heimlich on him. CAM pretends to choke it up once – twice – but then it is clear the noises are those of sexual gratification – BENNY is confused – CAM and TIMP start rolling about with laughter.

TIMP. We're having you on, you fucking spanner!

BENNY stands angry and red.

CAM. That was nice though – will you do it again?

TIMP. Aren't you lovely when you're angry – you're like a very troubled tomato.

BENNY. You're such a pair of – fucking – (*Growls.*)

TIMP. Ooo – look there's another one – Benny-boy? Lighten you up?

BENNY. Not before me cornflakes thanks.

TIMP. Well – in for a penny – in for a pound! (*Sinks the second pill.*) Benny, you're being a bit of a grumpy fucking frowner. Is it not a time of celebration? Did you not get your hexam results?

BENNY. Yes.

CAM. How d'you do?

BENNY. First.

CAM. Nice one, man.

TIMP. We shall have bubbles!! Bubbles for breakfast.

> TIMP *goes to the fridge and cracks open a beer and hands it to* BENNY.

BENNY. Cheers.

CAM. Cheers!

BENNY. You done any practice?

CAM. Not much.

BENNY. Shouldn't you /

TIMP. Will you two stop fucking bleating – tell him about last night, Cam!

> TIMP *has put on some pretty serious dubstep.*

BENNY. Timp, man?

TIMP. Oh come on!

> TIMP *puts on 'Keep Young and Beautiful'. He starts grooving around the place a little.*

You want to hear what happened last night then?

BENNY. Will you stop blinking like that you're making me feel ill.

TIMP. First, a toast.

BENNY. What are we toasting?

TIMP. You. I fucking love ya, ya grumpy brainy faggot!

CAM. Aye-aye.

BENNY. Cheers.

TIMP. World of work, Benny-boy, just you wait till you start – it's like lighting a match – sort of exciting for a minute then you realise you can't un-strike it – so there's nothing else to do but get up at dawn every fucking day and wait till it's burnt! Ha!

TIMP lets out a wild laugh right up in BENNY's face – BENNY smiles.

Just saying, buddy – beginning of the fucking end!

BENNY. Thanks, Timp. Thanks.

TIMP. Here is to a beautiful bloody rainbow.

They put their cans up.

BENNY. Contract's up at the end of the week we should think about clearing up, getting out. Maybe tomorrow we should /

TIMP. Tomorrow, tomorrow – I'll love yaaaa… don't go and summon the fucking evil 'Leprechaun of Dawn', Benny-boy!

BENNY. Leprechaun of Dawn?

TIMP. Tomorrow says you are giving in to the God of morning, saying it's okay for him to come and shit his horrible daylight all over us, tearing us apart. No one says tomorrow. Them's the rules or the Leprechaun of Dawn will arrive and stick his pointy teeth into your horrible little wrinkly bollocks and nibble them off.

BENNY. Right. Glad I cleared that up.

CAM. To tonight!

BENNY. What's tonight?

CAM. My concert is done, you guys have your results – and Timp... doesn't need an excuse – we thought we'd have a party; a sort of end-of-an-era thing.

BENNY. To tonight.

The three boys raise their cans and drink.

TIMP. Gluggedyglug. Now, yesterday – however, is a different matter altogether.

BENNY. Can you try and be less –

TIMP. Less what?

BENNY. Just. Less.

TIMP jumps up onto the table and starts to pretend to be walking down the street, a little like a Victorian gentleman, tucking his thumbs into his boxer shorts as if they were trousers.

TIMP. No. So – young Cameron and I are in George Square having a gentlemanly peruse of the prospective students of the gentler gender, wondering if they might like a more mature hand to guide them through this troubled time of change – were we not, Cameron?

CAM. We were.

BENNY. You two tour guides for students?

TIMP. Yes indeedio.

BENNY. Neither of you went to the fucking university.

CAM. We know the basics.

BENNY. How?

TIMP. We've seen you go to lectures.

BENNY. Fucking hell.

TIMP. I snaffled myself a garment –

CAM. He nicked a T-shirt from the university shop.

TIMP. Split the tour guide in two – cocks to the right, tits to the left – I'll take the left.

CAM. Ta very much.

TIMP. And we set off on our merry way. Four hours later and Cameron arrives home –

CAM. Having spent all fucking afternoon fielding questions about the rugby team and Greyfriars fucking Bobby /

TIMP. Miserable little mutt.

CAM. One of the pricks said 'Do you hactually know anyone who's hactually Scottish?'

TIMP. But when he arrived home much to his delight the flat was overfloweth – with young tail. Was it not, Cameron?

CAM. Aye it was.

TIMP. And were you not eternally grateful?

CAM. I had half a pint and went to sleep because I've got a very important concert.

TIMP. As if you did. Now we arrive at the rub.

BENNY. I'm not sure I want to know about your rub, Timp.

CAM. Listen, eh – this is so fucking cool, right – so /

TIMP. Wait, wait – the youth are so hasty. We'll get to it. So, she's called Margaret /

CAM. Megan.

TIMP. Was it not Mégane – like the car?

CAM. Like a Renault Mégane?

TIMP. No, you're right – it was Megan. I think – anyway – she's hot, right? Impressive honkers – long hair, big eyes – lovely looking; she's Australian or something –

CAM. Austrian.

TIMP. She's Austrian.

BENNY. Right. Is this /

CAM. And she's quite funny – actually, you know, a laugh – but a bit loud.

TIMP. And she's so fucking excited by the prospect of us –
she's all over Cam, right /

BENNY. *You* got laid?

TIMP. Don't be daft. / So we get back here and –

CAM. What the / ?

TIMP. Don't sulk.

CAM. I get laid /

TIMP. Don't lie /

BENNY. Carry on!

TIMP. And we're all in here. Beers out, smoking a bit – music –
all these fucking girls, I mean fuck knows what we were
talking about but you know they were excited and we were
experienced and they liked my dancing and it was, all in all a
lovely atmosphere. You know, sort of a crèche, sort of a
stable, sort of heaven – and this Renault girl – she's sixteen,
seventeen maybe – just done her Highers, straight into uni –
stands up and says 'I'm a virgin. I don't want to start
university a virgin. Will one of you have sex with me?'

CAM. 'Please' – I distinctly remember her saying – please. I
remember thinking… good manners.

BENNY. Whoa. Sixteen.

CAM. It's not that young.

TIMP. All things are relative, Cameron.

CAM. And she's pissed.

TIMP. Not that pissed.

CAM. Pissed enough not to notice that earlier Timp had put his
cock in her pint whilst she was telling a very interesting
story about Kirkcaldy.

BENNY. Who fucked her?

CAM. He just plopped it in there – like a fucking water snake
and she's telling this story with this pint in one hand and
everyone's fucking killing themselves – I mean – really

laughing and she thinks it's because of her bus-stop story and everyone's really screaming about Timp's magnified fucking bell-end.

TIMP. Magnified my arse.

CAM. Poor cow. And when she turns to look he's wopped it out and put it on her shoulder – everyone's still screaming right – now she's confused so /

BENNY. She's pissed, your cock's in her pint and she's sixteen –

TIMP. Seventeen – maybe.

BENNY. She's a pissed teenager!

TIMP. Moral fucking dilemma right?

CAM. No – I think he means /

BENNY. You fucked her?

TIMP. But she's standing there and she is pretty, and she is legal /

BENNY. Timp!

CAM. And she did say please.

BENNY. Who fucked her?

The door slams open and MACK *enters, he is latently thunderous – silent – somehow completely impervious to the action that he's walked into.*

Beat.

MACK *starts making himself a cup of tea.*

Silence.

MACK. Morning.

CAM. You making tea?

MACK. Yes.

CAM. Can I have a cup?

MACK. I don't know – can you?

BENNY. Carry on.

TIMP. I'm late for work.

BENNY. I want to hear the end of the story.

TIMP. We'll tell you later.

BENNY. I want to know who /

CAM. Sugar please, Mack.

> MACK *hands* CAM *a cup of tea.*
>
> *Beat.*
>
> MACK *sits.*

BENNY. Cam – carry on.

CAM. I should be practising really – I /

MACK. Don't let me stop you.

CAM. I wasn't there for all of it.

BENNY. Spit it out.

> CAM *freezes.*

CAM. I don't really – I can't remember – very /

> MACK *starts to laugh.*

BENNY. Tell me who fucked the girl.

TIMP. May I?

MACK. You already were, weren't you?

> *Beat.*

BENNY. Timp?

TIMP. Room's silent – Mack stands up, walks over, takes her hand and takes her to his bedroom. She just goes with him, like he's fucking Obi-Wan Kenobi –

CAM. It was brilliant – fucking brilliant.

> CAM *slaps* MACK *on the shoulder.* MACK *looks at* CAM. CAM *removes his hand.*

TIMP. We don't see either of them for the rest of the night.
Alacazam – there it is!

Beat.

MACK *claps* TIMP*'s story.*

Thank you – thank you, kind sirs – I have been delighted to
have been your entertainment for this brief time but if I may
now –

MACK. Are you fucked?

TIMP. I think the question is, Mr Mackenzie – are you?

TIMP *sniffs* MACK.

BENNY. Are you?

MACK. Drugs, no – don't touch 'em.

BENNY. How old was she?

MACK *looks up from his tea. Beat.*

CAM. I swear that shite is starting to fucking crawl – it's doing
my head in – I can smell it from my fucking bedroom. They
said when they're picking it up yet?

TIMP. You're such a fucking drama queen. You fucking love it,
us all sitting here with our tongues out – come come on, how
old?

MACK. Haven't you got a concert to go to?

CAM. Later.

MACK. Shouldn't you be rehearsing?

TIMP *starts giggling.*

Something funny, Timp?

TIMP. Nothing.

MACK. Tell me, Benny – why are you looking at me like that?

BENNY. Like what?

*They hold the stare for a few second more – it is latently
aggressive.*

TIMP. You totally did – you're such a bad boy, Mack – such a bad – bad – bad /

MACK. And what exactly is it that you think is bad?

BENNY. Are you joking?

MACK (*suddenly grave*). No.

CAM. It's just funny cos – she's sort of, young and /

MACK. Seventeen.

TIMP. Did you draw her a map?

CAM. Yeah but –

MACK. But what?

CAM. You're twenty-three.

MACK. So? What's age, eh, Cam?

TIMP. Without anything to compare it to your cock probably looked quite big.

BENNY. She was a virgin.

MACK. We all were once.

TIMP. Bet she'll be a Pringle.

CAM. What's a Pringle?

TIMP. Once you pop you just can't stop. Has anyone got any chewing gum?

MACK *throws* TIMP *some chewing gum.*

TIMP *pours himself a glass of water and chugs it down.*

BENNY. It's wrong.

CAM. Has anyone seen my bow?

MACK. Why? Why is it wrong?

CAM. I think we're just saying it's a bit – you know, risky, I guess – she's –

MACK. Let's all be precise, shall we?

BENNY. You took advantage.

MACK *and* BENNY *hold the tension between them – there is a beat.* CAM *and* TIMP *try to recover over the top but it brews beneath.*

TIMP. Can someone please explain to me – why when you two are sitting there having just polished off four years a studying with shiny old marks and you – (*Pointing at* CAM.) are about to get your tiny magical musical arse kissed by half the world and we are going to have a blinding fucking knees-up – I am the only one that is having a lovely old time?

CAM. Because you had drugs for breakfast, Timp.

TIMP. Right.

CAM. I need to go for a slash.

TIMP. Oh – careful –

CAM. What?

TIMP. Nothing.

CAM *exits.*

Pause.

BENNY. She have any mates with her?

MACK. What?

BENNY. The girl, last night – she have any friends with her? Looking out for her?

TIMP. Right – tonight – I'll bring back the food – chip in for the booze – and I'll /

BENNY. Did she?

TIMP. Benny, we were having laugh? No need to /

BENNY. Wonder if she is, right now? Having a laugh with her mates – or maybe she doesn't have any up here yet, so she's just sitting on her own somewhere with a sore head and sore fucking – wondering what /

MACK. She asked calmly and rationally for someone to sleep with her. She had come to that decision on her own. To say no, would have meant that I thought I knew more about what was good for her than she knew herself. Now – I'd say that would be pretty patronising. No?

BENNY. Sometimes people don't know what they want.

MACK. So what – we should make their decisions for them?

BENNY. She was seventeen. You're twenty-three.

MACK. Seventeen-year-olds have brains.

TIMP. Not all of them. I didn't. Still don't.

MACK. They can get married, they can drive cars –

TIMP. They can ride, Mack.

MACK. If she wanted to, and she did want to.

BENNY. She'd never had sex before.

MACK. Are you saying she wasn't capable of making the decision?

BENNY. But you were in a position of –

MACK. Of what? Hm?

Beat – BENNY *doesn't respond.*

I don't expect anyone to take responsibility for me. I don't expect to take responsibility for anyone else. I think it would be patronising. That's very clear to me.

BENNY. She was vulnerable.

MACK. You can't possibly know that.

Beat.

TIMP. Come on, lads – calm down – party tonight – eh?

CAM *enters – stopping* BENNY *from leaving.*

At the sight of CAM, TIMP *suddenly remembers it's time to go and starts scurrying to collect his things.*

CAM. Timp?

TIMP. Cameron, my little angel – I'm a bit late.

CAM. I just went for a piss.

TIMP. That's nice.

CAM. In the bathroom.

TIMP. Best place for it.

CAM. Why is there a naked girl in the bath?

TIMP. She isn't going to have a bath with her clothes on, is she?

CAM. She laughed when I got my cock out.

TIMP *trying not to laugh.*

TIMP. How unkind.

CAM. And made me jump so I pissed all over myself in front of a naked girl who was already laughing at me.

TIMP. Your cock.

CAM. What?

TIMP. From the way you told it it seemed clear that she was laughing at your cock specifically rather than you – as a whole.

CAM. Was she from last night?

TIMP. No, no – she's from work.

BENNY. The restaurant?

CAM. Did you sleep with her?

TIMP. Now, listen – here's the thing – right – so actually, quite a interesting story – she's one of the waitresses –

BENNY. She works with Laura?

TIMP. Sort of –

BENNY. Fuckin' hell, mate.

TIMP. No but listen – right – (*Takes to the floor – charm a-go-go.*) She turned up after her shift, looking for some green – I had this Afghani stuff she was after. She doesn't speak much English though, Polish or something – but older – you know – late twenties –

MACK. Doesn't bother me what you do, mate.

TIMP. And she turns up when I'm in the bog, right? And it's been one of those days – burritos – so I've laid a pretty impressive pile in there – and it won't flush, you see? I've tried and I've tried and then there's a knock at the bathroom door. I open it and it's this nice Polish girl and I think she's going to come in there and think I've left it for her, that I'm the kind of man that might do that, leave a browny staring her in the eye – and I'm not that kind of man? Am I?

CAM. Why has your shite got anything to do with that girl in the bath?

TIMP. Well, that's this Polish girl innit?

BENNY. Why did she need a bath?

TIMP. No, no, you dirty bugger – listen.

CAM. Carry on.

TIMP. I say 'I'm really sorry – I've done a massive turd and it won't go away.' But she can't understand me, you see, no comprendez. So I'm in a bind? So I mime the situation – I do a little face and a little squat and I mime the flush a few times and then sort of try and show it won't go.

CAM. Looks like funky chicken.

BENNY. You did a poo-dance at a girl that doesn't speak any English?

TIMP. Well, she didn't understand either, right?

BENNY. But it was so clear.

TIMP. So I have to take her by the hand and I show her over to the toilet, I show her what I've done and then to show her that it won't shift I pull the chain, right?

CAM. Right?

TIMP. And the thing only fucking flushes, doesn't it? It just disappears. Ala-fucking-cazam. I turn to her and she's looking at me – wide-eyed like I'm a fucking freak. As far as she's concerned I just opened the door – did the funky fucking shitting chicken, then all proud showed her my turd and just flushed it away. Like a little ceremonial doo-daa, bet she thinks it's fucking cultural. Them British and their big shits – I bet she thinks – and I'm so fucking embarrassed, so overcome with shame, the only thing I could do – was –

CAM. What?

TIMP. I mean – it's obvious –

CAM. Is it?

TIMP. What else could you do – I had to kiss her. To apologise, to defend the name of the British gentleman in her head; it was basically an act of patriotism. All things considered – I slept with her – for Queen and country.

CAM. Right.

BENNY. And Laura?

TIMP. See – there was nothing else I could have done.

MACK. Clearly.

Beat.

TIMP. See – not that bad at all, mind you – not as funny as you shagging a nipper though. (*Beat.*) That's really fucking funny – (*Looks at his watch.*) and I'm really fucking late.

CAM. What about the – ?

TIMP *kisses the top of* CAM's *head.*

TIMP. I'll come back with food – and drink, but buy extra, alright?

BENNY. Shouldn't we start thinking about shifting this before we /

TIMP. What if we stayed.

CAM. What?

TIMP. Couple of them freshers said – last night – this place was on the list for them to come look round – move in, like – and I thought – fuck off – this is ours, this is where we have our fun, keep your hands off. (*Beat.*) Just cos you two are graduating – doesn't really mean anything has to change – right? We could just renew the lease – we could stay?

Beat.

BENNY. Our lease ends in a week.

TIMP. So – we'll renew.

BENNY. We can't.

CAM. If they haven't found new tenants yet.

TIMP. Mack?

> MACK *shrugs*.

> We do have a lovely fucking time?

> *Beat – a strange silence falls.*

> BENNY *holds his silence – several seconds pass – no one can respond.*

> LAURA *enters*.

LAURA. I thought you'd be at work by now.

TIMP. 'Ello.

LAURA. Hi, boys.

BENNY. Hey, Loz.

CAM. Hi.

LAURA. I left my spare swipe-card in your room and I left mine at work last… are you high?

TIMP. Took a pill by mistake when I woke up.

LAURA. How?

TIMP. Thought it was aspirin.

LAURA. You're a fucking idiot, I can just go and /

BENNY. I'll get it.

LAURA. What?

BENNY. You two – catch up.

TIMP. No, no – you wait here; I'll go and grab it.

> TIMP *exits*.

> *Beat.*

LAURA. You lot have a party last night then?

CAM. Yeah – some freshers' thing.

LAURA. Isn't it the end of term?

CAM. Prospective students – seeing if they want to /

LAURA. Spend four years getting fucked... yes please. You alright, Benny?

BENNY. Yeah.

LAURA. Were you at the party?

BENNY. No. I was out with Sophie.

MACK *stands, removes himself from the table.*

LAURA. She alright?

BENNY *nods.*

It happen here? (*Beat.*) The party – the party happen here?

MACK. Ended up here.

LAURA. Wish I could have come.

CAM. Ach, you didn't miss much –

CAM *opens the freezer to get some ice out – and finds his bow – he takes it out and hides it quickly.*

I was in bed early – big concert – you know /

LAURA. Oh my God yeah the big concert; my mum's got your face on her fridge. I put it there. She's so excited to know you – she keeps telling everyone – 'my daughter is friends with Cameron Robertson, you know, that wee musical lad' – were there lots of people?

CAM. What?

LAURA. At the party?

CAM. Yeah, few.

Beat.

LAURA. Be so weird won't it, you not all being here, not being able to pop round. Bet you'll be glad – no more fucking motormouth.

BENNY. Don't be daft.

LAURA. Maybe you'll all come back one day and visit and have a big reunion and you'll go round all the bits of the house – like old pictures and be like, I looked at that and – I was sick on that, and I – you know – and if Cam gets really famous maybe they'll put one of them blue plaques up on the wall and I can be like, I used to hang out with them.

CAM. Yeah.

LAURA. I used to look at my teddy when I was small and be like 'teddy, I wonder where you'll be when I'm ninety' and I used to think about him rotting and get really sad.

CAM. Oh.

LAURA. I'm just going to use the loo – tell Timp when he /

BENNY. Laura?

LAURA. Yeah?

BENNY. It's broken.

LAURA. Oh. Oh well… I'll use the one at work.

TIMP *re-enters*.

TIMP. Ready?

LAURA. Yeah.

MACK. Don't forget to let your bath out.

TIMP. Be an angel, Cam – let it out for me. Don't get in it though – it's filthy.

TIMP *laughs a little nervously*.

LAURA. What you doing having a bath, it's boiling?

TIMP. Fancied it.

LAURA. See you tonight, guys, can't wait!

TIMP. Come on.

LAURA. You've scratched your back, babe.

TIMP *and* LAURA *exit.*

Silence falls.

CAM *takes a toke on a joint that has been smouldering, it's long and deep.*

CAM. Better let that bath out.

CAM *exits.*

BENNY *and* MACK *are left alone – neither speaks – time passes.*

MACK *eventually gets up to leave.*

BENNY. I'd get in that bath straight after – have a good wash.

MACK *stops.*

Beat.

MACK *laughs.*

MACK. Toilet's broken of course.

BENNY. You'd have let her walk in?

MACK. Wonder if she'd thank you. Guess we'll never know, oh great protector.

Beat.

BENNY. Sophie was out last night.

MACK. Yeah?

BENNY. Drinking – dancing.

MACK. Sounds like a laugh.

BENNY. No – the kind that makes you think someone's probably a bit, you know… broken.

MACK. Could mean either though, couldn't it? Could mean fine.

BENNY. Could mean falling apart.

Beat.

MACK *stands up abruptly from his chair, it scrapes along the floor – MACK grabs as many of the rubbish bags as he can carry and storms out of the kitchen – the door slams closed behind him.* MACK *returns to grab another handful.*

What are you doing?

MACK. Moving it.

BENNY. Where to? You can't put it on the stairwell the other tenants will /

MACK. I don't want to sit and look at it.

BENNY. I'll call the council.

MACK. Fuck – I wish we'd thought of that when they stopped collecting. Will you ring the rest of the city at the same time and just let them know that they'd been ignoring the blindingly fucking obvious?

MACK *kicks the door open and throws the bags out of it into the hall.*

MACK *continues to move it all – aggressively – until all the bags are out of the kitchen.*

BENNY *gets out his phone and makes a phone call – the automated voice comes on and* BENNY *confuses it for a human.*

BENNY. Hello – oh.

He sits on the phone – he is clearly been asked to wait, we can hear the tinny sound of 'Greensleeves' or something similar.

MACK *exits.*

BENNY *sits. The sun rises – the tinny music plays.*

Scene Two

Hot orange summer sun cuts across the dust that lies thick in the air.

There is no birdsong; there is no breath – the heat sits.

CAM *enters.*

BENNY *watches from on top of the fridge.*

CAM *wears his tails ready for performance.*

CAM *holds his violin.*

CAM *checks for anyone in the kitchen, but he fails to see* BENNY.

CAM *walks over to the far wall and stands with his face to it, his back to the room.*

CAM *takes a large breath.*

CAM *tries to play – he is too nervous – he cannot.*

CAM *lets his violin and bow fall to his side.*

CAM *bangs his head against the wall three times.*

CAM *takes another large breath.*

CAM *lifts his bow and his violin.*

CAM *plays half a note, fails.*

CAM *bangs his head against the wall.*

CAM. Fuck. Fuck. Fuck.

   Beat.

   CAM *takes a pill out of his pocket and places it in the palm of his hand he looks at it – he is on the verge of taking it…*

BENNY. What you doing?

CAM. Fuck, Benny, you scared the shit out of me.

BENNY. Shouldn't you be off by now?

CAM. My palms are sweating – my fucking /

BENNY. Don't take that.

CAM. My room's too fucking hot; Mack's playing his music full fucking volume – outside everyone's in the sun, having a great time –

BENNY. Go to the college or the concert hall – they'll be quiet.

CAM. Stinks of fucking rubbish everywhere.

BENNY. You alright, Cam?

CAM. You'll all be having a party whilst I'm gone; getting the beers in.

BENNY. And you'll be making history.

CAM. All I can see out my window is fucking students – throwing flour and eggs all over each other. You seen how warm it is out there?

BENNY. You should go, mate, you don't want to miss it.

Beat.

CAM. Don't I?

Beat.

BENNY. Course you don't.

CAM. You just jump through the hoops and it works out – exams, degree – job – there's a path. There's no maybe – maybe not – or tonight's the fucking night. All on one moment, all on one person – fucking…

BENNY. You've got instructions.

CAM. What?

BENNY. The music – that's instructions, isn't it. Don't get that in an exam. (*Beat.*) Nice up here – like being above everything – you can control it, calmer – cooler somehow.

CAM. Cooler?

BENNY. Yeah.

CAM. You're on top of a fucking fridge, Benny.

BENNY. The top of a fridge is actually… I thought you were meant to be leaving?

CAM. I'll go in a minute.

BENNY. You're going to be late.

CAM. I've got ages. You want a drink?

BENNY. No thanks.

CAM. Come on – have a drink?

BENNY. I'm alright.

> CAM *picks up a ball and chucks it at* BENNY, BENNY *catches it.*

CAM. Come on – we'll chuck it about a bit? It'll help me calm down.

BENNY. What time are you meant to be there?

CAM. Don't know.

BENNY. Cam?

CAM (*snaps*). What?

BENNY. Go.

> BENNY *throws the ball back.*

CAM. It's easy for you – you've got a piece of paper saying you know it and that's that. Imagine if tonight I could just walk on stage and in front of that whole fucking crowd and just roll out a piece of paper and go – look – this says I can do it so there we go. And then everyone cheers and claps.

BENNY. It's just pressure – there's always going to be /

CAM. Exactly fucking right – it's always going to be there.

BENNY. You don't get to be excellent without there being pressure. It's a pay-off.

CAM. Who says I want to be excellent?

BENNY. Fifteen years of eight hours' practice a day.

> *Beat.*

CAM. There's this guy coming, tonight – he's a Russian virtuoso called Viktashev; he's come up from London. He's pretty much it – you know? The big balls.

BENNY. Nice.

CAM. And he sends me this email the other day – it's like two pages long, saying he's heard my stuff and how now is a vital time for me. How there's this competition in Belgium; it's called the Queen Elizabeth and it's, you know –

BENNY. The big balls.

CAM. Aye – and this Viktashev guy won it when he was nineteen, youngest ever – and he wants me to go and break his title. He says he's going to ship me over to Vienna and train me – just me and him. And he keeps going on and on about how there's this window, this right age – and if you can get through it – you'll go somewhere great but if you miss it – you won't get it back.

BENNY. You got to not listen to all that /

CAM. And then at the end he writes this little story about how the lowliest and youngest inmates in Russian prisons tattoo stars on their knees.

BENNY. Why?

CAM. To say they won't kneel to anyone.

BENNY. Bit much that.

CAM. I'm meant to do what he tells me and not do what anyone tells me – you know what I mean?

BENNY. Yeah, it's a bit much. Got to do it for you I guess.

CAM. If I was doing it for me I'd stay here and have a pint with you.

BENNY. Right. (*Beat.*) Can't waste it though, Cam.

CAM. Why not? My choice, isn't it?

BENNY. Right now I reckon I know more than I ever will again. Iteration, deconstruction, reification, homogeneity /

CAM. Show-off.

BENNY. I'm never going to use those words ever again. So I might as well not know 'em. It's a waste. You though, you'll go on getting better and better and you could be – great, you know? Like – really really get to the top of something – get close to – inch of God.

CAM. What?

BENNY. That's what my dad used to call it, 'inch of God', the extra inch that takes you from great to – really being the dog's fucking bollocks. You got a shot at that. Not to be sniffed at.

CAM. Don't sniff at the dog's bollocks?

BENNY. Do not, Cameron.

CAM. You can keep learning words – keep studying.

BENNY. Thanks.

CAM. PhD – teach or something.

BENNY. It's all criticism though… not sure that's something you want to be great at, is it?

CAM. Come up with your own ideas can't you?

BENNY. What's the point in following something hardly anyone else can follow? I reckon you just end up somewhere no one else is ever going to visit.

CAM. Hardly anyone is great at the violin.

BENNY. But everyone's got ears.

CAM. I don't want to do it.

BENNY. You have to.

CAM. I don't want to.

BENNY. I don't know if that really matters.

CAM. What?

BENNY. Bigger than you somehow; maybe.

CAM. It's my fucking fingers.

BENNY. You believe in God, Cam?

CAM. No.

BENNY. Not even in primary, like nativities.

CAM. Snow.

BENNY. What?

CAM. Imagine, a bit of snow right now – how good would that be?

BENNY. There's no snow in the nativity.

CAM. It's about Christmas.

BENNY. It's Bethlehem, it's red.

CAM. Alright, God squad.

BENNY. That's just geography. I miss it sometimes.

CAM. Geography?

BENNY. The idea of something above you. I used to imagine him just sitting up there at night-time, made you feel a bit safer.

CAM. You don't believe in him any more?

BENNY. Don't think so.

CAM. Why not?

BENNY. Learnt too much, I guess.

CAM. Can't you just decide?

BENNY. It's like you get two books by well-known people, credible people, out the library and they say opposite things but they're both meant to be right. What are you meant to do about that?

CAM. Choose one.

BENNY. Just like that?

CAM. Yeah – why not?

BENNY. Then you always know you chose it, so it's just a choice rather than a knowing.

CAM. What's the difference?

BENNY. You chose it – so you know can just un-choose it – flimsy. It's one option but it could have just as much been the other one, it's like TVs inside TVs – they eat each other – like all the facts sort of chase each other, round and round – all the articles and books and blogs and papers and journals and they just keep running round and round and – You remember *Little Black Sambo* –

CAM. Sounds a wee bit /

BENNY. It is – but that's not the point. It's this story where this little kid meets these tigers and he gives them all his best most colourful clothes so that they won't eat him and they like those fancy clothes so much they chase and chase each other so hard that they just melt into butter.

CAM. Tigers turn into butter?

BENNY. I guess I just miss – you remember when you had a question, any question easy or hard, you know – what's ham through to why are we alive – and you knew the absolute best place to get a right answer was your dad.

CAM. Yeah.

BENNY. When your dad was like Google but better and with hugs. (*Beat.*) You'll be alright. You've got to go though, you got to try – it matters.

CAM. Can't I choose not to.

BENNY. You've got to go – one of us – has fucking got to – I won't let you give up. I won't let this flat make you give up.

Pause.

CAM. I'm sorry, Benny.

BENNY. I just think you should try, that's all.

Beat.

CAM. But what if I do?

BENNY. What? What if you try? Then you'll know you did your best.

CAM. Exactly.

Pause.

BENNY. You're going to miss it.

CAM. Sometimes think I'd be much happier if I'd never picked the fucking thing up.

CAM picks up his violin and starts to pack it away, BENNY watches silently.

BENNY. Knock 'em dead?

CAM nods.

BENNY nods.

CAM exits.

BENNY looks at the kitchen, rolls his sleeves up and defiantly heads over to the half-emptied cupboard. With confidence he begins to put the things into a bin bag – he is full of confidence when –

CAM enters.

CAM. I cannie go.

BENNY. What?

CAM. The whole of the fucking landing is stacked up – I can't get out! I can't get out down the stairwell.

BENNY. What? It's not that many bags – it was only /

BENNY exits and checks the front door.

(*Off.*) Mack!

CAM opens a beer – looks at it – doesn't drink it.

BENNY re-enters.

How did that happen?

CAM. I don't know.

MACK enters.

MACK. What?

CAM. I can't get out the front door for all that shite you put out here.

MACK. Come on – it was only a few bags.

BENNY. He needs to go.

CAM. I have to go, I'm late!

MACK. Well – move it then.

CAM. I can't get past it to move it, it's at waist height.

MACK. That's not all ours.

CAM. No shit, Sherlock.

MACK. Well then.

BENNY. They clearly dumped it because we – you – did.

MACK. I put ours out there; there was more than enough room to get past.

CAM. Mack, it is a wall – I'd have to wade through it to be able to move it and I'm in a fucking suit already sweating my balls off, I shift that lot I'm going to stink like a rat's arse.

Beat.

BENNY. We'll help you.

MACK. Will we?

BENNY. I'll help you carry it.

CAM. Thank you.

MACK *shrugs. The kitchen door is wedged open and bags start flying in –* CAM *and* MACK *passing what seems like an endless stream of rubbish into the kitchen, bag after bag – in they come,* BENNY *works hard to try and find space for them but they start really taking up space, the kitchen starts to feel much smaller.*

BENNY. Go on – go. We'll sort it.

CAM. Thanks, Ben.

BENNY. Come back a superstar.

CAM. Do my best.

CAM *goes to leave*.

MACK. Cam?

CAM. Yeah.

MACK. Good luck, man.

CAM. Thanks.

CAM *exits*.

MACK *and* BENNY *stand and look at the rubbish*.

MACK. Council didn't answer then?

BENNY. It was automated.

MACK. Really?

MACK *nods*.

BENNY. Have you got something you want to say?

MACK. No, no.

BENNY. It is their problem; I mean it is their job to sort this out.

MACK. Okay.

BENNY. You pay for it to get picked up and the council pick it up.

MACK. Right.

MACK *goes to make himself a cup of tea*.

BENNY. I'll put it back out then.

MACK. We don't.

BENNY. What?

MACK. We don't pay for it. We're students, we don't pay council tax.

Beat.

BENNY. Cam and Timp aren't students.

MACK. They don't pay, that's why they live with us. That and cos we're fucking lovely to look at.

BENNY. Yeah fine – but we're still entitled to the same services.

MACK. Entitled?

BENNY. Deserve – we're /

MACK. We're – ?

BENNY. We're going to give it back… soon.

MACK. Oh right. Okay. Here's to hoping it gets better soon.

BENNY. What's the other option then?

MACK. Not saying there is one.

BENNY. You think we should get rid of it ourselves?

MACK. Can't see how we'd do that.

BENNY. Then what?

MACK. Then nothing.

BENNY. If we don't 'deserve' to get it picked up and we can't get rid of it ourselves – Mack? Then what are you offering, what are you – suggesting? You think we should eat it, fucking breathe it in?

MACK. Calm down, Benny.

BENNY. Stop acting like you've got a fucking answer.

MACK. No – no – I haven't got any answers, Benny, none at all.

BENNY *picks up several bags of rubbish and takes them out of the front door.*

MACK *makes his cup of tea, cleanly – almost rhythmically – from 'off' we can hear* BENNY *in the stairwell, he is having an altercation with someone. As first we can hear him speaking calmly – and then it bursts into a much larger, more aggressive argument.* MACK *listens to the argument and leans, nonchalantly against the counter.*

BENNY *comes back in with the bags that he was carrying.*

BENNY *looks at* MACK.

BENNY *puts the bags down.*

Tea?

BENNY *doesn't respond.*

Bicky?

BENNY. No.

MACK. I thought you were going to put them /

BENNY. Guy opposite's on the landing – he said I couldn't dump it out there.

MACK. Really?

BENNY. It's a common stairwell.

MACK. True.

BENNY. You want to live like this?

MACK. It's just trash.

BENNY. It's crawling – we can't get it out – we can't dump on the street, we'll get fined, we can't put it in the stairwell and no one is coming to pick it up – we're going to fucking drown. I don't want it in here. I shouldn't have to live with other people's crap all over me – we didn't make this mess!

MACK. I think you're getting things out of proportion, Benny.

BENNY. Am I?

MACK. I think you should breathe.

BENNY. I think you should try and be less of a selfish cunt.

MACK (*laughing*). You're the one that wants to post it back through people's letter boxes, piece by piece, Benny.

BENNY. I'm going to ring the landlord.

MACK. Oh yeah?

BENNY. They have to do something, it's a health hazard.

MACK. No they don't have to do anything – don't you see?

BENNY. No I fucking don't!

MACK. How many students do you think are moving out this week? You think they're going to let it cost them to move it, you kidding?

BENNY. We'll call the police.

MACK. Look out the fucking window – How many houses do you see? Hm? Ringing the council, ringing the landlord, going to have a gentle word with the neighbours – if there was a solution do you not think someone would have thought of it over a week ago when they decided to stop picking this shit up and it started rotting under our own fucking noses?

BENNY. Someone has to take care of it.

MACK. Who?

BENNY. They won't just leave us here to /

MACK. Who?

BENNY. Because that's how things work, there are people, organisations –

MACK. Who?

BENNY. Systems that make sure /

MACK. Who?

BENNY. This is Britain, you idiot, they won't just leave us to rot! It's not fucking /

MACK. I'd love to take a look at your world, Benny; I bet it's lovely.

Beat.

BENNY. I'm going to be out of here. I'll just leave it with you.

MACK. Where you going?

Beat.

BENNY. London.

MACK. Sounds expensive.

BENNY. Get a job.

MACK. Hear there's hundreds going.

BENNY. Got a first – haven't I?

MACK. Oh, you should have said – you'll be fine then.

Pause.

BENNY. What if I'm not?

MACK. What?

BENNY *comes in close to* MACK.

BENNY. What if I'm not fine – what would you do about it – pal?

Pause.

MACK. You got to learn to look after yourself, mate.

BENNY. You've been crying.

MACK. Red-eye – I had a joint.

BENNY. Your face is wet.

Beat.

MACK. Redemption.

BENNY *earnest – looks at* MACK *– long pause.*

MACK *starts to laugh a little –* BENNY *immediately defensive but unsure what is going on.*

Red. Dead. Redemption. I forget to blink when I'm gaming if I'm high. Sorry to disappoint.

BENNY *lunges at* MACK *and smacks the bottom of his cup of tea – the tea flies up and all over* MACK.

MACK *freezes a moment – looks at* BENNY.

Just trying to do you a favour – Ben, make sure you don't fall too far.

Beat.

BENNY *goes to leave as he does so the kitchen door opens,* SOPHIE *enters.*

SOPHIE. Hello.

BENNY. Sophs?

SOPHIE. Hey. (*Kisses* BENNY *on the cheek.*) Mack.

MACK. How did you get in?

BENNY. You get home alright last night?

SOPHIE. What?

MACK. Who let you in?

SOPHIE. The door was open.

BENNY. Must have bounced off when I slammed it.

SOPHIE. Bloody hell – it's worse in here than it is out there.
  Why don't you put it in the stairwell?

MACK. Not very neighbourly.

SOPHIE. Having all this in here in this heat isn't good for you.

BENNY. We know.

SOPHIE. Well, you need to move it.

MACK. What would we do without you?

SOPHIE. I'm not being funny.

BENNY. Sophie – we realise /

SOPHIE. You know you have to pay.

BENNY. What?

SOPHIE. Can't settle the strike so private companies have
  stepped in in the interim. We have to pay to get it picked up.

BENNY. How much?

SOPHIE. Tenner a bag.

BENNY. What? No way.

SOPHIE. Everyone has to pay.

BENNY. What the fuck? Ten pounds a bag – they're taking the
  piss.

SOPHIE. Cheaper than dumping it if you get caught. One of the boys next door to us, they were trying to clear out their flat and he gets a two-hundred-quid fine for dumping a bag not in a communal bin – but the bins are fucking rammed, there's no space left in any of them. It's an infringement of civil rights.

MACK. What, the inalienable right to dump your shit on someone else?

SOPHIE. He had no other choice.

MACK. He could have paid to have it picked up.

SOPHIE. He might not have the money.

MACK. Then he should make less mess.

BENNY. Mack?

SOPHIE. I can see you've done really well at keeping it to a minimum.

MACK. Everyone starts dumping on the streets and it's chaos in seconds.

SOPHIE. Everyone keeps it in their houses and you get illness that costs as much as the clear-up would.

MACK. Got any stats on that? Sounds pretty spurious to me.

SOPHIE. Spurious? That's a complicated word, Mack.

MACK. What are you going to do with yours then, Little Miss /

BENNY. Mack – back off.

Beat.

SOPHIE. We moved out yesterday. I leave tomorrow morning.

MACK. What? Why? (*Realising he's betrayed himself.*) Bet Daddy came and sorted it all out for you.

SOPHIE. Yes.

Beat.

BENNY. Fuck, Sophs – you can't just leave.

SOPHIE. End of term, isn't it. I'll be back for graduation – can I get a glass of water?

BENNY. It'll be weird not – um – you're going to London though, right – so, we'll all still /

SOPHIE. Of course. Course we will.

Pause.

BENNY. I'm going to go and check the contract – see what it says about deposits. You alright in here?

SOPHIE. Yeah I'm alright.

BENNY *exits.*

'How did you get in?' What was that?

MACK. Better I ask than Benny.

SOPHIE. Just say you lent me your spare keys.

MACK. Why would I have done that?

Beat.

Guess I'd better have them back.

MACK *hands* SOPHIE *her water.*

SOPHIE. Thank you. I don't –

MACK. You're going – tomorrow?

SOPHIE. Why did you cancel last night?

MACK. Had to.

SOPHIE. Why? It's none of my business what you do.

MACK. Cam and Timp ended up bringing a party back – I couldn't – um –

SOPHIE. Right.

SOPHIE *tries to give* MACK *the keys.*

MACK. Keep 'em.

SOPHIE. What for?

MACK. I don't know – just – keep them.

Beat.

SOPHIE. I could put them back in your room for you.

Beat.

MACK. I said keep them.

SOPHIE. We could watch a movie.

MACK. He's getting /

SOPHIE. What /

MACK. Shaky.

Beat.

SOPHIE. Aren't we all? (*Beat.*) We can have a joint – just – talk and /

MACK. You want tea?

SOPHIE. I've got water. (*Picks up her glass of water.*) Pussy.

SOPHIE *pours the glass of water down her front, it makes her T-shirt go see-through.*

Shall we have a nap?

MACK. No.

SOPHIE. What are you scared of?

MACK. Nothing.

SOPHIE. You're terrified.

MACK. Women love to tell men how they feel, don't they?

SOPHIE. Men?

SOPHIE *looks around trying to see one.*

MACK. Think you've 'interpreted' something – think you've discovered a feeling, think you can stick a flag in it – own it, irrespective of whether it's total bullshit or not.

SOPHIE *stares at him.*

SOPHIE. Have you got a boner?

MACK *turns away from her.*

MACK. Fuck off. I haven't got a fucking /

SOPHIE. Why turn away then?

MACK. I'm making myself – a – piece of /

SOPHIE. Cock.

MACK. Biscuit.

SOPHIE. A piece of biscuit – what's that then?

MACK. I'll smack you in a minute.

SOPHIE. Oh yes please.

MACK. Right –

MACK *turns back around.*

SOPHIE. Careful you'll have my eye out.

MACK. Come here –

SOPHIE *backs off.*

SOPHIE. No – no, Mack.

MACK *crouches and prepares.*

Benny'll come in.

MACK. I'm just taking the trash out.

SOPHIE. Take that back.

MACK. No!

MACK *lunges at* SOPHIE *and gets her over his shoulder easily – she screams – MACK panics – and puts her down quickly – 'shhing' her all the while.*

Shh-shh.

SOPHIE (*serious*). Take that back – I'm not trash.

Beat.

MACK (*looks at her – humble*). You're not trash.

    Beat.

    BENNY *enters.*

    SOPHIE *reacts as if* MACK *has just poured water right down her front.*

BENNY. What the fuck's going on?

SOPHIE. He just poured water all over me!

BENNY. What? Why?

SOPHIE. He just fucking drenched me!

BENNY. What are you doing?

MACK. She – it was a joke.

BENNY. What the fuck is wrong with you?

MACK. I thought she was going to /

SOPHIE. Will you get me a T-shirt please, Mack?

    MACK *exits.*

BENNY. I'm sorry.

SOPHIE. It's fine.

BENNY. He's been a cunt ever since /

SOPHIE. No he's not.

    Beat.

BENNY. Dad sent his love – hoped you were alright. Said you should pop by if you're ever /

SOPHIE. Yeah – yeah.

BENNY. Said he'd like to see you.

SOPHIE. Mm – it's really fucking hot, Ben.

BENNY. Yeah.

SOPHIE. Excited about tonight?

BENNY. Can't wait.

    MACK *enters.*

MACK hands SOPHIE the T-shirt, she turns away from BENNY and MACK to put it on.

We got them T-shirts in Amsterdam.

MACK. Yeah.

Meanwhile we see SOPHIE smell the T-shirt. She seems small, soft for a moment.

Beat.

SOPHIE. What does it say in the contract?

BENNY. It has to be cleared before we can leave or they take our deposits; six hundred quid each.

SOPHIE. That's outrageous – they can't /

BENNY. And under Scottish Law it's joint responsibility – one of us doesn't pay and everyone else and their guarantors are responsible. Looks like we're in it together, eh, Mack?

Beat.

MACK. I'd double check the signatories.

BENNY. What?

MACK. Front page.

BENNY reads the front page of the contract.

BENNY. You're not fucking on here? What the fuck?

MACK. We turned the sitting room into my room – remember?

BENNY. You don't live here.

MACK. Never liked contracts.

Pause – BENNY sees the keys on the floor.

BENNY. They your keys, Mack?

MACK. Oh yeah – must have dropped them.

BENNY. You alright?

SOPHIE. Fine, why?

BENNY. You look a bit… has he been having a go?

SOPHIE. No.

BENNY. Don't let him.

SOPHIE. I'm alright, Ben.

Beat.

BENNY. You remember last night, Sophs? It was so hot out –
you could have taken your shoes off, carried them like flip-
flops. Everyone out, everyone with their skin out – all
having finished exams – all smiling and high-fiving – and
saying hi to all these people, fucking hugging them – people
I've seen every day for four years, people who have seen me
– and I'm hugging them thinking – I've got no fucking idea
what your name is. Four years, seeing them every day – and
you still don't even know their fucking name... hardly know
them at all.

Beat.

BENNY *walks over to the window to look out.*

SOPHIE *and* MACK *look at each other – unseen by*
BENNY.

We'll throw it out the window – fuck it, we'll just throw it
out the window.

BENNY *tries to push the sash of the window up.*

BENNY *tries again –* BENNY *looks up at the window lock.*

MACK. They're locked.

BENNY. What? Since when?

MACK. Landlord didn't want any more accidents.

BENNY. I didn't give the say-so –

MACK. Your dad did.

BENNY *stands, lost – confused, overwhelmed, he bites his
finger.*

Scene Three

The surface of the kitchen table has been cleared. Around the kitchen are the remnants of food preparation, pots, pans – there are yet more rubbish bags piled around the circumference of the room. The lights have been switched off, there is only evening gloom from the window – it is nearly dusk. Along the length of the table lies a body covered in a black sheet.

Behind this MACK, SOPHIE *and* BENNY *stand.*

SOPHIE *is dressed as Snow White,* BENNY *is dressed as a lion. They are blindfolded.*

In front of the body, on the opposite side of the table to the other three, stands TIMP, *dressed as Peter Pan.*

TIMP *climbs up onto a chair.*

TIMP. One –

The three prepare to take their blindfolds off.

Two –

TIMP *lights a match and it burns brightly in the dusky light.*

Three. You were blind but now you can see!

SOPHIE, MACK *and* BENNY *take their blindfolds off – the light from* TIMP'*s single match half-illuminates the gloom.*

There is an intake of breath.

BENNY. What the fuck is –

SOPHIE *and* MACK *take a step backwards as if a little haunted.*

TIMP *holds the match up close to his face – the three stare at him – not being able to quite see the body in front of them.*

TIMP. What lies before you here, my friends, is a land of untold dreams, it's everything you ever hoped for, everything that flickered behind your lids on a lazy afternoon – and it can be yours, all yours – you just have to reach out and touch it. So be brave, my little warriors – steel yourselves for an onslaught of pleasure like you have never considered before

– a battle of loveliness, a skirmish of delight – arm yourself
with your weapons – and prepare to devour – the lovely – the
jubbly – oo – oo fuck – ouch –

The match has burnt down and TIMP *starts waving it about
manically trying to stop it from burning his fingers – the
match goes out – all is dark.*

BENNY. Timp – what the hell is /

BODY (*in an intentionally spooky deep voice*). Hello.

TIMP *turns the lights on.* BENNY *pulls the black sheet off
from over the body, there is something hopeful in his face.*

TIMP. どうぞめしあがれ [*Pronounced: Douzo meshiagare!
Meaning: Help yourself!*]

What is revealed is LAURA *in a makeshift Little Mermaid
outfit, covered from head to toe in carefully placed sushi. She
has chopsticks in her hair, soy sauce in her belly button and
wasabi and ginger in either palm.*

LAURA. Hiya!

SOPHIE. Is that sushi?

LAURA. No, it's me, you idiot.

TIMP. It's the best fucking sashimi dream you ever fucking
dreamt, right? Am I right? We got maguro, ikura, saba, ebi –
and sake!

SOPHIE. What the –

TIMP. Tuna, salmon roe, mackerel, shrimp and salmon –

LAURA. I'm like a mermaid –

TIMP. It's a marvel.

LAURA *sings a few lines from 'Part of Your World' from
Walt Disney's* The Little Mermaid.

BENNY. You've got soy sauce in your belly button.

TIMP. Fucking great, right? Come on – dig in. There's
chopsticks in her hair /

LAURA. Ginger in my right hand and wasabi in my left.

TIMP. Chuck us some beers, Mack.

MACK *turns to the fridge to get the beers.*

BENNY *wanders over to the window – TIMP passes him a plate and it falls to his side. BENNY stands apart, looking out at dusk across the city.*

SOPHIE. This is amazing; this must have taken hours.

TIMP. Why do you think you lot have been stuck in my room playing dress-up – talking of which, Mack, where's your fucking costume?

MACK. I'm wearing it.

LAURA. I can't see him what are you wearing? Timp, will you tell me what he's wearing?

TIMP *goes to get* BENNY *from the window.*

TIMP. Come on – tuck in, Benny – poor cow's been there for ages already.

BENNY. I'm alright.

SOPHIE. Are you naked?

MACK. She's got a bikini on.

SOPHIE. Alright, hawk-eye.

MACK. No harm in paying attention to detail.

TIMP. There is when that detail's my girlfriend.

MACK. You dressed her up like a fucking goldfish.

TIMP. Everyone else has dressed up, mate? Look at him – fucking Simba over there.

BENNY. I'm Mufasa actually.

TIMP. Party's a funny time to have a gob on, that's all.

MACK. I'm fine.

TIMP. Come on!

MACK. I said I'm fine.

TIMP. Just come and have some food.

MACK. Don't much like sushi.

TIMP. What music do you fancy?

LAURA. Can we have some Disney – for the theme – can we?

SOPHIE. As if Timp's going to have a bunch of Disney tunes on his /

LAURA. He's got loads. He's got all the movies as well.

SOPHIE. What – why?

TIMP. You're asking a recreational drug user whether he likes multicoloured talking animals? Fucking love 'em.

BENNY (*still over by the window*). There are loads of white vans – driving down Princes Street.

SOPHIE. It'll be the rubbish collection.

BENNY. There's fucking loads of them though.

TIMP. What is wrong with you all?

LAURA. I'd dance with you, babe – if I could stand.

BENNY. Will someone help her up?

TIMP. She's dinner.

BENNY. She's clearly uncomfortable.

LAURA. I'm fine.

BENNY. She's not – she can't see anything or eat anything.

MACK. She said she's fine.

Beat.

BENNY. The sunset – it's made the whole city – pink.

LAURA. Red sky at night shepherd's delight – red sky in morning, shepherd's warning.

TIMP. We'll let the shepherds know – Come on, Ben – come eat.

BENNY. You can see it slipping; last tiny fraction of it.

SOPHIE. This is really good, Timp.

BENNY. Can't be going far though, eh? Stays fucking light all night – drives you mental. You reckon it hides just below the /

MACK. Benny?

BENNY. Yeah?

MACK. We're having a laugh.

BENNY. Are we?

MACK. Yep.

BENNY. What's your costume?

MACK. I'm Tinkerbell. I've just got very tiny wings. I'd prefer it if you didn't draw attention to them – I'm pretty self-conscious about it.

Beat.

TIMP. Look! Fucking look at that – (*Spots a crumpled up old ironing board under all the mess.*) You remember this?

SOPHIE. Tobog-ironing!

MACK. The tobog-iron!

LAURA. I can't see – show me!

No one shows her.

Timp – can – we, can I /

TIMP. Calton Hill – fucking king of the slopes on this bad boy; could have gone professional.

LAURA. That was the night we had the snow party.

SOPHIE (*sings*). Snow-body does it better!

TIMP (*kissing and playing with* LAURA). You got your little party-Nazi out.

LAURA. Can I get up now?

MACK (*robot voice*). 'Dance. Dance, everybody dance or I'll kill you, what's the point of a party unless you dance. Ahhhh, do not sit down, I will annoy you. Do not sit down, I will annoy you.'

SOPHIE. Wasn't the only thing you got out.

LAURA. Oh God don't.

SOPHIE. If you don't dance I'll get my rat out!

LAURA. What can I say? I'm a woman of my word. Please can I get up? Timp, it's starting to itch.

SOPHIE. Right in the middle of the dance floor.

TIMP. That you did, I was so proud.

SOPHIE. Benny, didn't you get off with Cat Logan that night?

BENNY. Did I?

> BENNY *walks over – silently whilst the hubbub goes on around him and he begins to take all the sushi off* LAURA. *There's something gentle about it – he removes it all – plates it all up and helps her up to her feet. When he's done –* LAURA *looks at him a moment – kisses him on the head, he nods at her.*

SOPHIE. She'd come dressed as the devil – which made no fucking sense, bless her – and was completely covered in red paint.

TIMP. Fuck – yeah I remember this. It was fucking brilliant! Cam had taken those mushrooms and was going all spacky trying to lift up the carpet looking for little people. Little people! Oooh, little people – you remember that, Mack? (*Suddenly pointing to* MACK.)

MACK. Fuck off.

TIMP. We're at – at – aaa fuck where was it, it was brilliant –

MACK. Massa.

TIMP. We're in Massa – sittin' in those booths, you know – all dark – and this one is fuck-faced – and he's talking to this girl. She's like, you want to come home with me – Mack's all – yeah yeah – so she shimmies out of the fucking booth and his eyes nearly pop out – she's only a fucking little person – a dwarf – she was tiny – very fucking funny that was.

SOPHIE. Benny – don't you remember you got off with Cat Logan in the shower and all her body paint went everywhere?

MACK. Cam burst in here – turns the music off and is like 'There's been a murder! There's been a murder in the shower!' He fucking believed it too – look on his face.

BENNY. That wasn't Cam. It wasn't Cam that took the mushrooms and ran in, it was /

TIMP. Then you walking in looking like you'd gone five rounds with a fucking Rottweiler.

LAURA. Which basically you had. Cat Logan is a dog, no two ways – she fucked Mike Elliot and tried to use Scotch as lube.

MACK. Fuck off?

TIMP. He had to go to A+E. Stingy todger.

LAURA. Poor wee guy – worst thing about it was it was a bottle of Balvenie twelve-year-old his dad had got him for his twenty-first. If I were him I have spent the next three weeks sucking on my bedsheets.

TIMP (*sings*). Once, twice – three time a laydeee – and I looove you!

LAURA. Fucking Balvenie twelve-year-old, you know what that costs?

TIMP. Who wants more disco biscuits?

TIMP *starts handing out pills*.

BENNY. It wasn't Cam that ran in.

TIMP. Come on, you!

BENNY. No.

SOPHIE. I remember you two meeting. It was in Stereo; we'd only just met you.

MACK. I met you at football.

TIMP. I remember thinking fucking students – bunch of fucking layabouts no thanks.

MACK. Right.

TIMP. Never done an honest day's fucking work.

SOPHIE. Anyway – you looking across the bar and going 'Oh shit – that's it – I'm fucked.' I took a step back cos I thought you meant you were going to be sick.

LAURA. You said that?

TIMP. Can't remember.

SOPHIE. I remember it exactly – you said it like there was nothing you could do about it. It was amazing.

LAURA. Oh, Timp. That is, Timp – that is /

TIMP. Alright alright it's not fucking Jeremy Kyle.

BENNY. We have to get rid of this.

TIMP. I told you we're waiting till we all come up – we'll be like twenty times faster. We'll have it all done in no time – all of us lot – if we're high, five minutes, tops. Like Billy Whizz.

MACK. Billy the Kid?

TIMP. Billy Whizz – the fucking Beano.

MACK. Who's Billy Whizz?

BENNY. All of us – we have to all lift it, because I can't – not on my own.

SOPHIE. You alright, Ben?

MACK. He's fine.

A pissed, hazy drunken hum continues – dancing, laughing – MACK looks on, TIMP cackles and jokes – LAURA fawns over TIMP. As they get high – and smoke fills the room – it gets hotter and hotter – they start sweating, gurning, sweat pouring off them – it sweats, it thumps – laughing, smoking – sitting, eyes rolling. There is a sense that it could always be this way – nothing forward, nothing backwards – there is something utopian and yet claustrophobic, this should last for just long enough that we feel it may never change. BENNY just sits – looking at it all – feeling increasingly desperate.

CAM *enters, still in his suit – carrying his violin, he is excited – bursting with success. He looks at the scene – he seems so composed, so smart. For a moment the others do not see him – they continue to sway and stagger and for a moment it looks as if* CAM *might want to leave.*

BENNY. Cam! Cam! Cam! Cam!

CAM. Alright, Benny?

BENNY. How was it?

TIMP *spontaneously rugby-tackles* CAM *to the floor.*

LAURA. You look like a little penguin! Doesn't he look like a little penguin?

CAM *tries to get up,* TIMP *rolls around laughing –* CAM *can't help but laugh.*

Like he's on ice – look at him – trying to, it's like Bambi. Bambi!

CAM. What the hell happened in here?

TIMP. We're tidying; we're just at the bit where it gets worse before it gets better.

SOPHIE. How was it? How did it go?

BENNY *goes over and takes his hand – desperate to hear him speak.*

BENNY. Tell us it went okay.

MACK. Anyone want another beer?

BENNY. Will you tell us?

SOPHIE. Give him a second.

CAM. God – it's nice to be back here. It was fucking intense.

BENNY. Will you tell us?

TIMP. Go on then – tell us how it went, you little homo.

CAM. It was – pretty amazing. I've never – I was really fucking nervous but… I don't think I've ever seen that many people – I mean except for football matches, but…

BENNY. Did you play well? The stars – the guy with the stars on his knees – the Russian – did he – did you impress everyone? Did they clap?

CAM recounts the evening but there is something about his passion, his excitement that cools everyone else a little – as if he has brought a draught in from outside.

CAM. I was so fucking nervous, I kept having to dry my hands, I swear I was actually sweating through my fingertips and I was so worried I was going to... but you know waiting to walk out there and you can just about see all those people and the lights are real bright and – fuck, my heart's still beating like the fucking – and you stand there and you see the glint on glasses and the odd grin but not much else so you're not really sure that they're there and – they start clapping and man – that many people – and the noise, the noise was so loud it make the stage shake a little bit, I felt it through my feet, the clapping, it was mad. And all the moisture goes out your mouth and suddenly you're standing in front of them and it's dead dead silent and – that was sort of the best bit – just when I was about to play and my bow is just a wee way off the strings – just waiting there – hovering – and it's there and you're still and then you hear this little tiny noise, this little fucking seat creak and you realise that fucking hundreds of people just leant in – just a fraction – to hear what you're going to do next – waiting for you to start.

Beat.

TIMP. You did your thing?

CAM. Aye – I did my thing.

TIMP. Big old hoo-ha after?

CAM. Aye – big old hoo-ha after.

TIMP. Well there we go – lovely jubbers. Pass me a beer, Mack.

Everyone goes back to their own business – CAM stands a moment, unsure whether to join in. BENNY sits still looking at CAM wanting more.

MACK. What am I a fucking vending machine?

TIMP. Well if you will stand by the fridge.

LAURA. Come dance – Cam.

LAURA *grabs him and spins him round and round, then puts him down and wanders back to* TIMP.

CAM (*almost shouting*). Everyone fucking talking to me and offering me shit and that guy – the Russian –

SOPHIE. Oop – exotic.

CAM. He wants to teach me – one on one – in fucking Vienna – I don't even know where that is!

TIMP. It's not anywhere near here.

CAM. They all stood and clapped and – it was – it was – great. It was really really great. (*Pause.*) You guys are totally fucked.

BENNY *nods*.

TIMP *hands* CAM *a rolled note and indicates a plate with coke on it.*

TIMP. Go on – get your snout in that, wonderboy.

CAM *does a line.*

BENNY *sees that* CAM *is a little disjointed – apart –* BENNY *goes to hug* CAM. CAM *steps back – takes his tie off and directs his attention to the rest of the group.* BENNY *stands alone.*

CAM. Let's fucking party!

LAURA. Are we going to get to say we knew you when you were younger when we're older?

BENNY *looks out of the window.*

BENNY. Cam, did you see what the white vans were? Cam?

CAM *parties in with the rest of them, not wanting to be left out.*

CAM. They're police vans.

BENNY. What? Why?

CAM. Don't know – they're parked right down Princes Street – helmets and batons the lot. Must be a march or something; fuck knows.

TIMP. Benny – come on!

TIMP *holds out a pill on his finger.*

Come on – gobble gobble.

BENNY. Why are there police vans? Is something happening?

TIMP. Come on – swallow some smiles.

MACK *still at one side watching* BENNY *all the time.*

SOPHIE *approaches* MACK – *drunk – dancing – being overtly provocative.* MACK *desperately tries to contain her – to shut her down.*

SOPHIE. Come on, grumpy – let's dance.

MACK *looks at* SOPHIE *with threat.*

Change the track, Timp.

MACK. I'm alright, Sophs.

SOPHIE. Come on.

TIMP. Batting above your average, Mack.

MACK. I'm alright – thanks.

SOPHIE. Don't make a girl beg.

MACK. Honestly – I'm –

SOPHIE *begins being pretty explicit with* MACK.

Stop it.

LAURA *catches sight and tries to pull* SOPHIE *away.*

SOPHIE. I'm mucking around.

LAURA. Sophs? Don't.

BENNY *catches sight.*

BENNY. I wouldn't touch him with a bargepole, Sophs – you might catch something.

TIMP. Bargepole? You joking? Toothpick more like.

SOPHIE. As if I would.

TIMP. I bet you're horrible in the sack, Macky.

MACK. Horrendous.

BENNY. I bet it's with his eyes closed and his teeth clenched and thinking furiously of his mother.

MACK. Spot on.

LAURA. You ever been in love, Mack?

TIMP. Ah, come on – as if!

MACK *starts to laugh.*

BENNY. Have ya – have you ever been in love?

TIMP. Only with toddlers.

SOPHIE. What?

CAM. Didn't you hear about last night? He fucked a seventeen-year-old.

Beat.

SOPHIE. You did what?

BENNY. Go on Mack – tell us.

Pause – the others, excited – willing MACK *to speak.*

MACK. You won't guess what Timp did.

SOPHIE *pours herself a shot and knocks it back.*

TIMP *glares at* MACK.

Timp was fucking hilarious he /

LAURA. What did you do, babe?

BENNY. Mack fucked a drunk seventeen-year-old. Didn't you, Mack?

SOPHIE. Did you? That's funny – God, Mack – what are you like?

MACK. I – I –

MACK *stands looking at* SOPHIE, *a glass in his hand not able to move.*

BENNY. Proud of it 'n' all – thinks he did her a favour, gave her what she asked for. Didn't ya?

CAM. She did say please.

SOPHIE. Oh, in that case.

LAURA. What did you do?

TIMP. I got my cock out.

LAURA. Boring.

SOPHIE. Was it good?

BENNY. Yeah – was it?

MACK *throws his glass against a wall and it smashes.*

CAM. Fucking hell!

MACK *laughs wildly.*

SOPHIE *stands stock still.*

TIMP *throws a bag of icing sugar all over* MACK.

TIMP *stares at* MACK, *the threat of violence is palpable.*

Beat.

They break – they laugh.

TIMP. You're a fucking mentalist!

MACK *gasping – gulping for air, still stares at* SOPHIE.

MACK (*snapping – wild*). You want to dance – let's fucking dance!

BENNY. Did it make you feel like a man?

MACK. Shall we – shall we! Turn it up – Timp – come on! Hey! You fucking remember – down south we went to Alton Towers for the day – we fucking remember this and I'm sitting next to Benny-boy – and we're waiting for this ride to kick off right and he's so fucking scared of this rollercoaster, such a fucking softy – he starts – he starts singing to himself – he starts singing – (*Sings a couple of lines from 'I Just Can't Wait to be King' from Walt Disney's* The Lion King.)

Fucking put it on, Timp, find it, let's dance – let's have a fucking dance!

TIMP starts looking for the track – CAM delighted by the hysteria starts leaping around with MACK – they start singing the song – MACK knows the words.

You remember, Benny – you remember how you cried?

SOPHIE. Stop it, Mack.

BENNY. You know the words.

MACK. Like a little lion all scared and /

BENNY. You took my hand and you sang it with me and you said I'd be alright – cos you knew I fucking hated heights.

There is a beat – MACK and BENNY look at each other for moment whilst the dancing leaps around them, there is something impossibly tender about it – but MACK can't stomach it – he belts out another line of the song. Pandemonium ensues – MACK drags everyone into the song – they are all singing. MACK gets to SOPHIE who looks up at him intensely – with one arm he pulls her up and close to him so their faces are almost touching – and he shakes his head to say 'no' –

No one else sees this – MACK then turns her away and carries on chanting for people to get up and dance. He is wild, untameable – a chant begins that sees him leaping from chair to chair – the distances are dangerous, the act is daring.

ALL. Mack! Mack! Mack!

He leaps.

BENNY *stands apart, silently watching.*

BENNY. It wasn't Cam that ran in from the shower...

MACK. Come and dance – Benny-boy.

ALL. Mack! Mack! Mack!

He leaps.

BENNY. I don't want to dance.

ALL. Mack! Mack! Mack!

He leaps.

BENNY (*louder*). I don't want to dance!

ALL. Mack! Mack! Mack!

He leaps.

BENNY (*louder still*). I don't want to dance!

MACK *tries to leap a final time but he has arrived at the chair that has not yet been touched.* MACK *goes to leap and he can't – he can't touch it – everybody stops – the moment is too great to ignore.*

Beat.

I want to know why my brother killed himself.

Lights down.

Scene Four

It still isn't dark – the husky blue of twilight lingers in the air. Debris from the party can be seen but the kitchen is empty, except for BENNY *who sits alone at the kitchen table. He gets up and goes over to look out of the window.*

CAM *enters – he's still in his shirt from the concert but has now paired it with shorts.*

CAM *lingers by the door.*

BENNY. Eh-up.

CAM. Hi.

BENNY. Y'alright?

CAM. Yeah.

BENNY. Where you all hiding?

CAM. Bathroom. Not hiding – just they wanted a bath. Cold water or –

BENNY. Probably figured lions don't like water, big cats, aren't they?

CAM. What?

BENNY. Nothing.

CAM. It's nice, it's like kids – we're doing bubble beards. You should come.

BENNY. I'm alright.

Beat.

CAM. Those pills were shit, eh? Can't feel a thing – Timp reckons they're duds. Everyone's mellow as fuck.

BENNY. I guess there's a mood.

Beat.

CAM. I wanted to say thank you.

BENNY. What for?

CAM. Earlier – for making me go.

BENNY. You would have gone anyway. You seen this?

CAM. Are there more than earlier?

BENNY. Yeah – been building all night; hundreds of them. (*Beat.*) Exciting, Vienna though – great that is. Only way is up. It's good.

CAM *comes over and looks out the window with* BENNY.

CAM. What are they doing? They're just standing there.

BENNY. I saw one of them earlier, pop his baton under his arm and lift his visor up and eat a whole fucking hot dog.

CAM. So?

BENNY. Why do you need riot gear to eat a hot dog?

CAM. You don't.

BENNY. Then why are they wearing it?

CAM. I don't think he put it on just so he could eat the hot dog.

BENNY. I know that, you flaming idiot.

CAM. What's your point?

BENNY. Why are they there if there's no riot?

CAM. Waiting for one I guess.

Beat – CAM *looks out of the window a moment.*

They'll fuck off home when they run out of hot dogs.

BENNY. Makes me angry.

CAM. Don't let it.

BENNY. You sure those pills were shit?

CAM. What?

BENNY. You're gurning like a bloody washing machine. Here.

BENNY *gets a piece of chewing gum out of his pocket and gives it to* CAM*; he puts his fingers on either side of his jaw and starts to massage it.*

CAM. Probably just a bit tense.

BENNY. Oh yeah?

CAM. I wanted to ask you something, Benny?

BENNY. What?

CAM. It's stupid really.

BENNY. Go for it.

CAM. It's tiny – it's just – after the concert –

BENNY *finishes massaging* CAM*'s jaw and ruffles his hair.*

BENNY. There you go, munchalot.

CAM. We were talking at a table after the concert, me and Viktashev, right? And he's saying all this stuff about how exciting things are going to be and how I need to watch out because everyone is going to want a piece of me –

BENNY. Did he put his hand on your leg? I'll fucking kill him if he did.

CAM. No – he didn't put his hand on my leg.

BENNY. He put his hand on your cock?

CAM. No – (*Laughing*.) listen –

BENNY. It's no fucking laughing matter – I'll chop his cock off, if you need someone to –

CAM. No. No – listen, I'm being serious.

BENNY. Shame.

CAM. This old guy comes over to us. He's got this camera. He's dressed like an old-school artist – this silk-scarf thing and the soles of his shoes were thick and his coat was heavy, you could tell it had been really expensive. (*Beat*.) He says 'Viktashev?' He's Russian, I think, Eastern European anyway. Viktashev seems not to recognise him – but the old guy asks if he can take our picture. Viktashev looks at me with his eyes wide and he raises his eyebrows and then he turns to the old guy and he says 'no thanks'. Like fucking wincing and smug – (*Imitates*.) 'no thanks' and then, I think, he adds something like… buddy. Then Viktashev turns his head away from the old guy's face really quickly and laughs a bit and smiles at me and his eyebrows go again and he says 'so where were we?' like he and I were on the same team against this old guy. But I didn't want to be on Viktashev's team. You know what I mean?

But the old guy didn't move – he just stood there, looking at us, then he starts rooting around in his bag. Viktashev gets a bit loud and says 'look' – with this hard 'k' that makes the old guy blink like he's startled – and a bit of Viktashev's spit lands on this old guy's coat, but the old guy just keeps blinking and rummaging and Viktashev again 'look' – with the hard 'k' and buddy – 'we're having a meeting'. Like the old guy couldn't see we were having a meeting? And I wanted to smile at the old guy to tell him it was alright but who the fuck am I to try and smile him out of the situation? So I don't smile at him and I just look at the table.

The old guy eventually finds this book and takes it out of his bag and he places it on the table – and immediately Viktashev puts his hand on it and I see that Viktashev's

wedding ring is new, really shiny and clean and I – somehow
that makes me think – 'what the fuck do you know?'
Viktashev tries to push the book off the table – but the old
guy doesn't even notice, he's got his thumb wedged in
between two of the pages and he's opening it and I realise
it's his like album, his portfolio – and he's smiling because
he thinks the second we see it we'll understand, so he's
smiling. Viktashev is calling for security and I can see photos
of all these ballerinas that I think I recognise and an actor
and musicians, and then right at the end there's fucking
Picasso, this amazing photo of him – when he's just about to
start painting, the paintbrush is like seconds away from the
canvas – it's class – and I think, fuck me, this guy's taken
Picasso's photo.

Beat.

BENNY. Did security come?

CAM. Aye but before they got there the old guy just smiles –
he's got yellow squares for teeth, really square like Travel
Scrabble pieces, the little magnetic ones, no letters though,
obviously – anyway – I say – 'I think they're really good.'
(*Beat.*) Benny – who the fuck am I to say – 'I think they're
really good'? I'm a fucking kid compared to him. Why isn't
anyone looking at him? He's taken Picasso's fucking picture.
He's done a whole life. (*Beat.*) What would you do if
someone told you – if you knew – if the look in some old
guy's face told you that being young was as good as it ever
fucking gets?

Beat.

BENNY *looks at* CAM. BENNY *doesn't respond.*

*There is an explosion outside the window – it's dulled by
distance but we can feel it.*

ACT TWO

Scene One

There is an explosion outside the window – it seems closer now, the room shakes.

BENNY. What the fuck was that?

They both go to the window to look out.

CAM. It's burning.

BENNY. Fucking hell.

CAM. Fuck – that policeman's on fire – look at him. Look.

Beat – they stare.

How did... (*Stops himself from asking the question.*)

BENNY. Police vans don't just explode.

CAM. Must have overheated.

BENNY. Engines were off, been there for hours. No way.

CAM. Then /

BENNY. Don't know.

Orange light continues to reflect through the window – the police van burns.

CAM continues to chew, it's manic, it's tense.

Take that fucking gum out, man... you're killing me.

CAM. I'm going to tell the others.

BENNY. They won't care.

CAM exits.

BENNY stands at the window. BENNY climbs up on top of the fridge. In the distance we can hear CAM telling the others about what has happened, no one enters.

Long pause. BENNY *looks out of the window.*

We can hear laughter from off.

BENNY *sits.*

TIMP *enters, he is looking for weed, he finds some and sits at the table and begins to roll a joint.*

TIMP *doesn't see* BENNY.

LAURA *enters soon afterwards and sits down next to him.*

LAURA *goes to go and look out of the window.*

LAURA. You seen the /

TIMP. Come here.

TIMP *beckons* LAURA *to him and she immediately goes over, forgetting the window completely.*

LAURA *rests her head on* TIMP's *shoulder whilst he rolls.*

LAURA *doesn't see* BENNY.

LAURA. It's nearly midnight.

TIMP. Hm.

LAURA. Why don't you ever tell the boys?

TIMP. They're usually away on holidays this time of year; never understood the fuss anyway.

LAURA. You want water?

TIMP. I'm alright.

LAURA *doesn't move.*

You not having any?

LAURA. Just wondered if you wanted it, that's all.

Pause.

You were talking in your sleep Monday; really badly; couldn't sleep at all.

TIMP. It's just dreams, eh.

LAURA. Shouting, kind of – like you were shouting at something. You grabbed me.

LAURA *shows* TIMP *the mark.*

TIMP *kisses the mark.*

TIMP. I'm sorry.

LAURA. You were asleep, eh.

TIMP. Yeah, but still.

Beat.

LAURA. It's horrible to watch, your face all screwed up, grinding your teeth. I can't take my eyes off you when you're like it – it's like a baby in pain or something.

TIMP. I can never remember a thing.

LAURA. Seems unfair.

TIMP. Why?

LAURA. Don't know – guess just, me having to watch you – just – you know, waking up after, fresh as a fucking daisy, not remembering.

TIMP. I can't help it.

LAURA. I'm not saying it's your fault – I'm just saying it doesn't seem fair, that's all.

TIMP. I'm asleep, aren't I?

LAURA. I know, I know. It's just – it's like there's an earthquake and you're right next to me but you're sleeping right through it and making me hold up the whole room on my own.

TIMP. I'm fucking asleep, Loz.

LAURA. I know – It's just weird, that's all – it doesn't matter.

TIMP *lights the spliff and starts smoking it.*

TIMP. I'm sticking to myself.

LAURA *goes to the sink and makes a towel wet, she lays it on* TIMP*'s forehead.*

LAURA. You ever think I should be a bit more…

TIMP. What?

LAURA. Sophie's sort of – sophisticated, isn't she?

TIMP. Is she?

LAURA. Yeah. I think so.

TIMP. She's from the south; southerners think their shit's sophisticated.

LAURA. I think you're sophisticated.

TIMP. That's because I am.

Beat.

LAURA. You ever think about what you'll be like when you're old?

TIMP. No.

LAURA. I sometimes look at the back of my hand and wonder what it will look like when it's all wrinkly. Like that same bit of skin right there, and either I die first or that will definitely happen – you ever think about that?

TIMP. It'll be different skin.

LAURA. Look at it though, imagine – isn't that weird?

TIMP. No.

LAURA. It's weird that there's no way round it.

TIMP. I'll buy you some hand cream.

LAURA. I remember being like ten and being naked on my bed and looking down at my flat little body and imagining what it would be when there were tits and pubes and things.

TIMP. Things?

LAURA. Tits and pubes. And thinking it was the weirdest thing that they would just be there. No other option; you know what I mean?

TIMP. I've yet to grow into my tits.

LAURA. Imagine all your tattoos; you'll look like a page of writing that's been rained on.

TIMP. Thanks.

LAURA. Timp?

TIMP. Yeah.

LAURA. I'll still love you; even when you're smudged.

TIMP *smiles at* LAURA, *gets up and goes and refills his glass.*

Them all graduating, makes you wonder, doesn't it?

TIMP. I hate this.

LAURA. What?

TIMP. When you get all, you know, thinky, in the middle of the fucking night. It does my nut in. Where is everyone – it's not even fucking midnight – why we given up so early?

LAURA. Shut up, I'm being clever.

TIMP. No you're not – you're being a pain in the arse.

LAURA. Doesn't it make you think about what you'll be – one day, when you're old?

TIMP. No. It makes me glad I've already got a job and didn't waste twenty K on a fucking useless degree.

LAURA. You know how I have a smoke every now and then – but, I wouldn't say I was a smoker though, would you?

TIMP. Laura? I love you very much.

LAURA. I know.

TIMP. But will you shut the fuck up?

LAURA. No listen, if you just smoke every now and then for ages well then you must actually become a smoker at some point and I wonder when that is. If it's an age or a time or – like I never intended to be a waitress, it was just something I was going to do for a bit until I stopped and did something proper and I just wonder when I stop being someone who was going to be a waitress for a bit and I just become a waitress. I don't want to be your wife and a waitress… for example.

TIMP. Stop thinking. It'll hurt your head.

LAURA. I think Cam might be really famous; my mum stuck his face on our fridge. I don't think I'd want that.

TIMP. Well, that's lucky cos you don't play the fucking violin.

LAURA. I know it's not very – I don't know – it's just, I only ever really think about being really good at being a mum. (*Beat.*) I know I shouldn't say that, but I don't know, somehow that seems like enough. Like it's really important, somehow. Don't know why. I'd like to make a home for us. Is that weird?

Beat.

TIMP. No.

LAURA. I sometimes wonder how Sophie feels, knowing that she wasn't enough to stop him. You know?

TIMP. Yeah.

LAURA. I'm going to make a cuppa; those pills have made me head hurt.

LAURA goes over to the kettle.

TIMP. Not sure a cuppa'll fix that.

LAURA. Give it a bash, eh? Timp?

TIMP. Yeah?

LAURA. Would you like to move in with me?

TIMP looks up at LAURA in silent shock.

Some time passes.

TIMP. Not yet eh? When we're a bit older… maybe.

LAURA. Just thought I'd ask. In case… doesn't matter though.

Unseen by TIMP she gets a tiny cupcake and a candle out of the cupboard.

LAURA puts the candle into the cupcake.

TIMP. I'd die without you, babe.

TIMP exits.

LAURA. I know, you big dildo.

LAURA *lights the candle and turns around to give* TIMP *the cake – but* TIMP *has gone.*

LAURA *stands – crestfallen – behind the candle light she sees* BENNY *on top of the fridge.*

LAURA *freezes a minute – unsure of what she's seen.*

BENNY. Hiya.

LAURA. Buggery wank fuck, Benny. You scared the life out of me – you shouldn't do that.

BENNY. Sorry.

LAURA. How long you been up there?

BENNY. I dozed off. Door woke me.

LAURA. I thought you'd gone to bed.

BENNY. Couldn't sleep.

LAURA. You want a cup of tea, babe?

BENNY. Yes please.

BENNY *climbs down.*

BENNY *sits and watches* LAURA *making tea – there is something calming about her.*

You looked out the window?

LAURA. No.

BENNY. Police van – exploded – burnt out. Twitter says they've arrested someone.

LAURA. Oh no. Where's your mug?

BENNY. Over there. Laura?

LAURA. Yep.

BENNY. You think it's more important to be honest or to be happy?

LAURA. Milk?

BENNY. Thanks.

LAURA. Sugar?

BENNY. No – thanks.

LAURA. I don't think I've ever made you a cup of tea before, isn't that funny?

Beat.

BENNY. But if –

> LAURA *stops making tea for a moment and comes over and holds* BENNY*'s head in her hands, she kisses the top of his head and gives him a big cuddle.*

LAURA. I think we're quite similar you and me, Ben. Need things feeling safe before we can rest. Otherwise you get so anxious in your tummy, you know – so sort of scared, need things to feel, level.

BENNY. Yeah.

LAURA. Horrible innit, when it's all all over the shop?

BENNY. But?

LAURA. You know what I do. I – I have this picture in my mind of how things are going to look when they're all sorted; I sort of make a safe place in my head. Like me on a sofa with fluffy slippers, don't know why they're fluffy but they are – and Timp with his hand on my head, like he does, and us watching the TV and whenever things are looking a bit grim – I just focus really hard on that picture and I know that whatever happens now, doesn't really matter in the long run – just so long as I eventually get to that sofa – you know what I mean?

BENNY. But how do you know you're going to get there?

LAURA. Cos I can see it. I wouldn't be able to see it if it weren't real, would I?

BENNY. What if you lose your picture? If a bit of it breaks.

Beat.

LAURA. Can't see how I could lose it, it's in my head, int it? Who can steal it from in there – you plonker.

> LAURA *passes* BENNY *his cup of tea and ruffles his hair.*

BENNY. But what if Timp /

LAURA. Stop thinking so much. It'll hurt your head.

BENNY. Laura?

LAURA. Don't, Ben.

Scene Two

SOPHIE *bursts through the door; she's got a bubble beard on and is looking for someone, she doesn't find them… she's laughing – excited.*

SOPHIE. Hi.

LAURA. Hey.

BENNY. I'm going to try and get some sleep.

SOPHIE. Oh no – come and play – look at my beard!

BENNY. It's brilliant. (*Beat.*) You seem so okay, Sophs.

SOPHIE. What?

BENNY. Everyone was so worried you'd… but actually you're fine.

Beat.

SOPHIE. I –

BENNY. I'm saying it's a good thing.

BENNY *exits.*

LAURA *still stands with her tea, relaxed.*

SOPHIE. You coming back through?

LAURA. In a minute.

SOPHIE *turns to leave – just before she exits.*

Sophs? Can you untwist my bra strap for me – it's digging right in and I can't reach it, keep trying and getting in a muddle.

SOPHIE. Sure.

SOPHIE *approaches*.

It's not twisted.

LAURA. Oh. It felt like it was.

SOPHIE. Nope – all fine.

LAURA. Who were you looking for?

SOPHIE. Hm?

LAURA. When you came in – you were looking for someone.

SOPHIE. Was I?

LAURA. It wasn't Benny or me.

SOPHIE. What?

LAURA. You looked like you hadn't found who you were looking for.

SOPHIE. Did I?

LAURA. Who were you looking for?

SOPHIE *finishes doing the bra strap – pause – they stare at one another.*

SOPHIE. I was looking for my cardigan.

LAURA. Oh, it's here – I saw it earlier – one sec.

SOPHIE *stands, itching to get away* – LAURA *locates the cardigan and goes to hand it to* SOPHIE. SOPHIE *comes in to take the cardigan.*

SOPHIE. Thanks.

LAURA *doesn't let go of the cardigan.*

LAURA. You remember little Jenny that used to be round here all the time because she fancied Cam.

SOPHIE. Yeah.

LAURA. You remember how she'd play football with them in hot pants and sit and play computer games for hours.

SOPHIE. Yeah.

LAURA. The boys were like – 'so what if she likes computer games and tiny shorts – what's wrong with that.'

SOPHIE. Yeah.

LAURA. And we found it so mad that they were all totally blind to her high jinks, silly wee cow.

SOPHIE. What you getting at, Loz?

LAURA. Just she'd forgotten that boys might not speak girl – but she's forgotten we could spot it a mile off.

Beat.

LAURA *gives* SOPHIE *her cardigan.*

SOPHIE *takes the cardigan.*

SOPHIE. Thank you.

LAURA. I know we only really know each other because of the boys but – you're my friend. I consider you – my friend.

SOPHIE. You're my friend too.

LAURA. When our dog died my mum didn't shed a tear but went straight out and bought five goldfish and she fucking hates fish.

Beat.

SOPHIE. It's not a reaction.

LAURA. It probably doesn't feel like a /

SOPHIE. It's not. It's real.

LAURA. It probably feels like it's /

SOPHIE. I promise you. It's /

LAURA. It's just that… Benny, if he knew – saw – I don't know, what he'd do. It's not a small thing, Sophs.

SOPHIE. It's not a bad thing.

LAURA. Isn't it?

Beat.

SOPHIE. The first night I knew – um – the first – he – Mack –
    came to my flat – we spent nearly nine hours straight just
    talking. I'd never done that, with anyone – before. We sat on
    my roof, we had two big bottles of beer and two cigarettes and
    we shared them both. It was really warm – and we laughed, so
    much. You know the kind where tears and snot and everything
    is coming out of your face and your stomach and your cheeks
    hurt from it – and you barely breathe. We sat and watched the
    birds in the sky all night – it never got dark – the sky stayed
    the most amazing colour… completely clear and this purple
    blue, like a really light bruise – and the birds were so black
    against it and squawking and he does a great seagull
    impression. At about three – we walked through the meadows,
    just the two of us – the city was so quiet, like all the shadows
    were left from the night but the light was already there for
    morning, like the two shouldn't meet but they had and it
    created this other world, this amazing other place – which you
    can only see if you keep your eyes open for that long – a gap
    in the net – a slice of time that isn't day or night but some
    other… and he looked at me and I felt like it might eat me
    whole, and I knew – I knew right then, somehow I knew – that
    everything in the world would seem smaller from then on.

And then we started singing – (*Sings a line of 'Ain't got No/I
Got Life' by Nina Simone.*) you know?'

LAURA *nods*.

We sang that and ran about until all the purple had bled out
of the sky and there were postmen – and then he had to go. I
went to kiss him and he said no – I had to make my choice
first.

LAURA. Choice?

SOPHIE. That night was the happiest I've ever been.

LAURA. It was before /

SOPHIE. We were singing and singing and running and –

LAURA. Sophie?

SOPHIE. What if it's bigger? What if it's bigger, more
    important than /

LAURA. Are you out of your mind?

SOPHIE. Why can't it be?

LAURA. Because someone died.

SOPHIE. That night – how I feel is *so* /

LAURA. Mack fucks anything that moves. He fucked a teenager last night, for God's sake.

SOPHIE. No he didn't.

LAURA. He did.

SOPHIE. He told me he didn't.

LAURA. Oh, well, in that case.

SOPHIE. Maybe I'm different – maybe what we have is /

LAURA. Sophs.

SOPHIE. Timp fucks people all the time and he still loves you.

Pause.

LAURA *takes a step away from* SOPHIE.

MACK *enters.*

MACK *goes straight over to the window, the girls remain silent.*

MACK. They've arrested that spacky pair of Goths from Princes Street Gardens for the police van.

SOPHIE. Really?

MACK. According to Timp according to Twitter.

LAURA. Bound to be bullshit.

MACK *turns back into the room.*

MACK. Anyone want a beer?

LAURA. No.

LAURA *exits.*

MACK. What's wrong with her?

Beat.

SOPHIE *stands and stares at* MACK – *she begins to sing 'Ain't Got No/I Got Life' by Nina Simone quietly into the silence of the room.*

In the distance we can hear drums beating – the muffled sound of loudspeakers. SOPHIE *continues to sing.*

Stop it.

SOPHIE *continues to sing.*

Stop it.

SOPHIE *continues to sing.*

Stop it!

Beat.

SOPHIE. Do you; have you ever actually felt any – guilt? Because it's come as a bit of a surprise that um, that – you, one, I don't, can't actually feel it. Like I can't get my body to do it, on its own, it's not something I can generate somehow, like, I – I find myself having to actually summon it, trying to encourage myself, to summon it and even then I can't do it, really, I can't feel it. I thought it might be shock at first and then – grief or but I think I might not feel it. I can't. I don't. All I can feel is total joy, total – peace. I look at you and I sometimes actually make myself think of him, I force him into my head and I don't feel guilty. What does that mean? What kind of person does that make me? (*Pause.*) Hm? Sometimes I think it's because – what we have is love, meant to be. (*Laughs.*) That we love each other, yes, Mack, that is what I sometimes think. Is that ridiculous? And sometimes I even think that that love is so important that it is bigger, or equal to – what he did. That they are just two feelings, one is love and the other is despair and both just have an action. And that those actions are different but that somehow they are equal – does that make me a monster? I sat at his funeral looking at his parents and Benny but all I could think of, all I could feel – was you.

But then I look at you and I wonder if it's actually there. I wonder if I added up the amount of minutes, hours, fucking days I have spent thinking about you, the amount of fucking longing I have done – if I added that up and weighed it against anything you have ever actually said… and – (*Pause*.)

But then you do the smallest thing you make me a cup of tea when I don't ask, or you touch my hand really lightly in a room full of people and I think no, Sophie, don't laugh – don't laugh because it's real and it's so much more real because it's unsaid and unspoken and un – un – un – it's so much more real because I can't touch it, because we can't say it and I can't see it, it's so much more real because I don't know if it's there.

Pause. MACK doesn't say anything.

Please say something. (*Pause*.) Please. Please tell me if…

She trails off unable to try any harder.

MACK *stands,* MACK *stares at her.*

MACK *does not,* MACK *cannot speak.*

A foghorn sounds loudly outside the window – the drum beats rise – the people are marching.

Scene Three

MACK *and* SOPHIE *stand, as before.*

The drum beat rises.

BENNY *charges in – excited, breathless.*

BENNY. They've fucking arrested that pink-haired fairy and the lanky fuck that sit by the bandstand.

No response.

For the van.

MACK *and* SOPHIE *look at him.*

There's no way it was them. No way – I've seen her spend fifteen minutes trying to get into a bag of crisps. There was no one but cops round those vans.

MACK. Alright, Poirot.

BENNY. It wasn't them.

MACK. So what if it wasn't?

BENNY. Two people just got arrested for something they didn't do.

SOPHIE *stands by the window looking out.*

MACK. Big deal.

BENNY. Something we know they didn't do.

MACK *gets himself a beer and ignores* BENNY.

It's wrong.

SOPHIE. There are lights coming down Lothian Road – torches.

BENNY. I'm going out there.

MACK (*lifting his beer above his head as if it's a sword*). By the power of Grayskull! (*Simulates fireworks and explosion akin to He-Man's transformation.*) I am the power!

BENNY *joins* SOPHIE *by the window.*

BENNY. Listen… you can hear drums.

TIMP *charges into the kitchen wielding a mop or something similar.*

TIMP. For the honour of Grayskull!

MACK (*in backing-track whispers*). She-ra, She-ra!

TIMP. I am She-Raaaaaa!

MACK. I am the power!

TIMP. What needs saving?

LAURA *wanders in after* TIMP. *She sits herself silently up on the side, almost unnoticed.*

BENNY. They arrested those Goths for the police van – they never did it.

TIMP. For the honour of Grayskull!

BENNY. I'm going out there.

TIMP. What? You can't.

BENNY. Why not?

TIMP. For the honour of Grayskull!

SOPHIE. There are drums – can you hear drums.

MACK. It's just the Kilted Celts down by the museum.

BENNY. It's nearly midnight – what they doing up at this time eh?

 CAM *enters*.

CAM. What's going on?

SOPHIE. There's torches and drums.

CAM. No way – it's the Cavalcade? I fucking love the Cavalcade.

BENNY. It's the middle of the fucking night – no it's not the Cavalcade, you dumb fuck.

TIMP. We could have the Cavalcade in here!

BENNY. It's people – they're marching.

CAM. Can we?

TIMP. Course.

LAURA. Timp?

TIMP. Now – first things first – what's a fucking cavalcade?

CAM. Oh.

BENNY. They're marching with all their rubbish – look! Fucking look! They're getting rid.

LAURA. Timp?

TIMP. Yeah, babe?

LAURA. Will you come home with me please.

TIMP. You poorly?

LAURA. No.

Beat. TIMP *looks at* LAURA, *he knows something is wrong.*

BENNY. There's hundreds and hundreds look – they're all carrying all their crap – they're carrying it, look, all those bin bags – looks like a massive shiny black beetle – looks beautiful.

TIMP. Sounds like it's all just about to kick off – why would we leave?

LAURA. I want to go home, Timp.

TIMP. Come on, babe.

LAURA (*stares* TIMP *dead in the eyes*). I know.

TIMP *freezes.*

BENNY. You coming? All of this – together, if we carry enough each – we can get clear of it – get tidy. You all coming?

Pause.

BENNY *looks at the room, they don't move – they're fucked.*

Yeah?

TIMP. Mate – I would – I just – Laura's feeling poorly and –

LAURA. No I'm not.

TIMP. We're having a nice time, aren't we?

BENNY. Mack?

TIMP. By the power of Greyskull!

MACK. I am the power.

Beat.

BENNY. My dad talks about back in the eighties – spent fucking months on the picket lines and the things they did, the fucking bile they used to shoot at the scabs for not being with them. You know? Really fucking get at them, try and pull them apart – cos they reckoned by just letting it go on – you were as bad as joining the other side.

TIMP. You've done it again, haven't you?

BENNY. What?

TIMP. Benny, how many times – eh? We've talked about it – haven't we?

BENNY. What?

TIMP. You've been watching *Billy Elliot* again – haven't you?

BENNY. Fuck off.

TIMP. You know what it does to you.

Laughter.

BENNY. We should be out there.

TIMP. 'I don't want a childhood – I want to be ballet dancer!'

BENNY. Can't you hear the drums?

TIMP *starts drumming on the table.*

You'll let everyone out there risk their arses on your behalf and you're happy to just sit back and watch it happen? Cam? You a coward 'n' all?

CAM. No.

LAURA. Timp – I want to go home.

TIMP *picks up* LAURA *and starts to ballet-dance with her.*

Put me down.

TIMP. Cheer up.

MACK. Choosing in here is just as much of a choice as choosing out there. 'Choose life – choose a beer – choose a fucking knees-up.'

BENNY. Amazing how in here doesn't take any fucking balls though?

MACK. You reckon?

SOPHIE. Calm down.

BENNY. Why? Why? I don't want to calm – I don't want to sit, I don't want to fucking drink or snort or fucking – I want to move.

TIMP. 'I want to dance.'

BENNY. I don't want to live like this.

MACK. Go on then! Get out – go and do it! Go and join the fucking masses.

BENNY. Don't you think that looks amazing. All them people – moving – not shouting or screaming – just marching – look – with all those bags, that many people deciding one decision at one time and them all saying it – really quietly – doesn't that – make your fucking, doesn't that make your heart beat a bit faster? Sophs – make your heart beat faster?

BENNY *bends down close to* SOPHIE.

SOPHIE. My heart?

BENNY. Yeah.

Beat.

SOPHIE. He's right – we can – move it all. If you guys go downstairs and check the street and then – a few of you in the stairwell and then – a couple of us – stay up here and –

LAURA. Couple?

SOPHIE. Whoever. Look after the flat –

LAURA. Which couple?

SOPHIE. We can pass it down to you.

CAM. I'll go down.

TIMP. On who?

CAM. I'll help you, Benny.

LAURA. Which two, Sophs?

BENNY. We all have to go; together.

SOPHIE. I can stay here with /

BENNY. All of us.

SOPHIE. We're having a nice time, aren't we?

MACK. You should go if you want to go. Go with Benny.

SOPHIE. Fuck you.

MACK *turns immediately on* BENNY *to disguise* SOPHIE*'s reaction.*

CAM. Whoa.

MACK. Why? Why together?

TIMP. Calm – down, Sophs – come here. Have a beer.

TIMP *hands* SOPHIE *a beer.*

BENNY. Because I can't carry it all on me own.

SOPHIE *puts some music on.*

Sophs?

SOPHIE. I'm too high not to dance, I need to dance.

LAURA. Timp – I'm leaving.

TIMP. No you're fucking not.

MACK. Let's have some shots – eh? Line 'em up, Timp – let's get involved.

SOPHIE. Involved? All of a sudden you want to be involved?

LAURA. I'm leaving.

TIMP. No you're not.

BENNY. I got caught smoking weed in sixth form. It were just one joint but the headmaster wanted to make an example of me right? I was up for expulsion. I wouldn't have sat my A-levels I would have fucking flunked – but – but do you know what my brother did? Sophie?

SOPHIE *stops and looks at him a minute.*

TIMP. Tequila – it makes you happy! Loz? See. Cam – get away from that window.

CAM. It looks amazing.

MACK. Cam! Come here.

BENNY. He convinced the entire year group to confess to having also smoked a joint that day. There was a queue – fucking fifty people long outside the headmaster's office.

What was he going to do – expel us all? We got an hour's detention each; that's all. Everyone – one hour's detention or I get expelled.

TIMP. Tequila?

BENNY. No.

TIMP. Sophs – get the lemons, hurry hurry.

SOPHIE *rushes to get lemons from the fridge.*

MACK. Lick 'em.

BENNY. Can't you see what I'm saying? It matters that there are numbers – it means we protect each other if we do it together – you see that?

Everyone licks the back of their hands.

MACK. Shake 'em.

MACK *pours salt all over the backs of people's hands.*

BENNY. Us sitting in here makes it more dangerous for them out there. Together we might get a little bruise – apart – we let one person fall completely.

Small beat.

MACK. Shoot 'em.

They all knock their shots back.

BENNY *grabs* SOPHIE.

BENNY. Don't you fucking care?

MACK *turns – savage and steps in the way.*

MACK. Let go.

BENNY. What does it matter to you? Every man for himself isn't it?

MACK. Let go of her.

BENNY. Why? She can take responsibility for herself, can't she?

Pause.

MACK *steps back – shrugs and walks away.*

SOPHIE *lunges at* BENNY *and goes to kiss him –* BENNY *flinches backwards and lets her go.*

What you doing?

SOPHIE *laughs,* BENNY *laughs nervously.*

MACK (*snaps*). Will you stop guilt-tripping everyone into helping you carrying your shit. You want to go and join your little gang out there – fucking go, Benny – but stop bleating. Because we're having a nice time – okay?

Beat.

CAM. I'll come with you – let's go. Let's do it.

TIMP. Oop – Bambi's got a hard-on.

MACK. He's making a fool of you, Cam.

BENNY. Come on – let's go.

MACK. Cam – there's no point.

SOPHIE. Let them go, right? If they've got the balls to fight for something they want – I say let them exercise their balls.

BENNY. Cam – go and check the stairwell, see how much we can get down and I'll start collecting it up.

LAURA. I'll come with you – let me get my bag.

TIMP. No one is fucking leaving! We're having a party – for God's sake it's not even midnight!

LAURA. Let me go.

TIMP. No!

CAM (*by the window*). The police – they're out the vans – they're stopping them, they've got fucking helmets and shields.

BENNY. They can't do that – not if it's peaceful – no one was doing anything.

CAM. They've stopped them; they're herding them like fucking cows.

BENNY. Come on, Cam.

TIMP. No one's fucking leaving – look, Sophs, turn the music up. Alright? (*Starts emptying it onto a plate.*) I was going to save it but – I've got fucking two hundred quid's worth of blow here. (*Starts desperately rolling a ten-pound note.*)

Who's in – eh? Fucking freebies. Let's go.

BENNY. Sophie? You with me?

SOPHIE *looks at* BENNY *a moment – turns to* TIMP *and does a line of coke.*

LAURA (*she's found her bag*). I'm coming with you – we'll go.

TIMP. I'm fucking three pills in – we're not ending this party! We're going till tomorrow!

BENNY. Cam?

CAM. One minute –

CAM *goes to do a line of coke.*

TIMP. You lot got any brains at all? You're about to walk out into a line of fucking coppers when you've each taken enough drugs to kill a small horse.

CAM *and* LAURA *stop.*

It's crawling with them out there. Curtains for your career, Cam; Loz, you've already had your hands smacked once.

BENNY. Who cares?

CAM. I don't want to get /

BENNY. You remember reading all that stuff in History or English about those lads going to war, Mack? Fucking sixteen seventeen some of them – I always sat and wondered if I would. I remember thinking, fuck – I'd like to know if I was the kind that would piss himself, or if I was the kind that would take on ten men and go out roaring – you ever wondered that? You ever wished you knew for sure – whether you're a coward?

CAM *looks at* BENNY *then up around the room.*

CAM. I'll go and check the stairwell.

CAM exits.

MACK (*comes in close to* BENNY). Well done, mate, just sent Cam to his fucking death – good pal you are.

BENNY goes to hit MACK and MACK ducks it.

Who you fighting, Benny-boy? Hm?

BENNY tries shove MACK it doesn't do anything to him – he stands strong.

TIMP. Strength of a bear, speed of a puma, eyes of a hawk.

MACK. I'm happy to roll up my sleeves but who are you fighting? The council? The landlord? The big bad government? The general fucking state of the nation?

BENNY. Fuck you.

MACK. Who do you think they're hurting – huh? You want to join those mindless little fuckers who haven't even begun to think it through – who?

BENNY (*pointing out the window*). At least they're doing something.

MACK. You are so much smarter than this, Benny.

BENNY. Am I?

LAURA goes to leave.

TIMP. Don't – Loz – please.

On the street outside there is an almighty explosion – we hear glass breaking, shouting – screaming – cheering.

MACK starts to laugh.

LAURA, SOPHIE and TIMP are over by the window.

LAURA. Fuck – they've just kicked in the window of the – fucking –

SOPHIE. They're throwing bricks. There's paint.

TIMP yelps with joy – he starts screaming, running up and down.

TIMP. That's the window of the bloody restaurant!

TIMP *picks* LAURA *up and starts spinning her round.*

That little firecracker down there just earned us a day off work, babe!

MACK (*to* BENNY). What you going to do? Go and kick the crap out of a shop window? Really feel like you're fighting 'the man' – when in fact, it's probably just a little old shopkeeper – that's worked his whole fucking life to build that shop up, and you'll kneecap him – in the name of what?

TIMP. We can wake up late and spend all fucking day in bed – I'll treat you like a princess, make you your eggy-bread you like – kiss your feet, use the old orgasmatron on your noggin, go to that posh coffee shop you like, I'll even read you a bit a *Harry Potter*!

MACK. Or are you going to go and wrestle with a cop? Except he's just doing his job; he's just a guy being paid to stand there. He doesn't give a shit about your problem, you think he's defending an 'idea' – a – a what? Why are you kicking him? Eh? Because I can guarantee you he's just thinking about his wife and kids and what he might have for breakfast. And he might put his fist in your face, but he's probably thinking about his brother or his dad – or the bloke his missus fucked whilst he was working late. It's just toddlers squabbling.

TIMP. Don't go home; babe – it'll all be alright in the morning, promise.

SOPHIE. They're throwing bricks, at the policemen.

MACK. You want to be part of that?

SOPHIE. They're coming into the street – they're trapping them in our /

LAURA. Cam's out there.

TIMP. Babe? Fucking day off – we're going have the best day ever.

LAURA *shakes her head.*

Don't make me come down on me own.

LAURA *puts her hand on* TIMP*'s face.*

MACK. Or are you going to fuck with a politician or a tutor – come on, tell me who am I hurting?

SOPHIE. Leave him, Mack. You've made your point.

MACK. Because this isn't anyone, do you see? This isn't a problem. The man that makes the decision to fuck you up doesn't know or care who you are and he probably doesn't have a choice.

SOPHIE. Leave him – Mack.

LAURA. Guys – Cam's out there.

MACK. He just has a boss and a wife and a wallet and he just pisses and wanks and cries like the rest of us, he's just cheap and scared and weak like the rest of us. So what is the point in fighting?

CAM enters; he's carrying bags of rubbish, he's shaken, almost crying.

CAM. The police are in the stairwell.

LAURA. It's okay.

CAM. They're afraid of fire. They told me to bring everything in off the landing. There's so much. I tried to tell him to go and fuck himself – to – say no but… I – I – didn't. He started asking me if I'd taken anything and I – I was scared.

Beat.

BENNY. But we can't take any more in here.

CAM. But he said /

MACK. We'll move it in.

BENNY steps into MACK*'s way as he tries to leave they stand close.*

LAURA grabs her cardi and runs with him.

TIMP. Loz? Don't – it's dangerous.

Just before he gets to the door.

CAM. You can't.

BENNY. What?

CAM. We have to stay put – we can't leave the building until they say so.

LAURA. We're trapped?

BENNY. I'll talk to them.

CAM. They're not letting anyone out. We've just to bring the bags in off the landing.

BENNY. Well, say no!

CAM. I'm sorry, Ben. I'm really sorry.

TIMP. I declare that a fucking lock-in! On top of a day off! Hoo – yeah!

CAM, downbeat, crushed – starts bringing the bags of rubbish in handful by handful.

BENNY stands and watches – the rubbish builds around him, higher and higher – it almost becomes a physical manifestation of BENNY's interior state; we are overwhelmed, we are trapped – there is no way out – we are going to suffocate.

BENNY (*calmly*). We have to try.

MACK. Why?

BENNY. We're students – we're the people who should /

MACK. Students, eh?

BENNY. What we have to say /

MACK. I was in a café few weeks ago – I see a professor marking exam essays – he flicks through three pages – doesn't even read 'em. Thinks for a minute chucks sixty-five per cent on the front; didn't even read it – Benny. People laugh at students – ethno scarves, drink too much – what you going to do – sew a little hammer and sickle on your army-surplus jacket? Eh? Fidel Castro T-shirt?

BENNY. We're the fucking future.

TIMP (*laughs*). I'm sorry, Ben – even I've got a have a little chuckle at that. You do sound silly.

MACK. What like him? (*Points to* CAM.) Good luck, mate. You know how old he is?

CAM. Shut up.

MACK. Anyone know how old he is?

LAURA. He's nineteen; it's in the paper –

MACK. Except he's not – he's twenty-one. Lied didn't you, Cam?

CAM. Shut up, Mack.

BENNY. That true?

MACK. Come on – no one cares. Tell 'em.

CAM (*really starting to get shaky*). Just leave me alone, okay.

MACK. Come on, pal, nobody minds – just tell 'em.

CAM. They put my age wrong in the paper – when I was ten – they said I was eight, my mum had written my brother's age by mistake and /

LAURA. You're not actually the youngest ever violinist in the Royal Scottish /

CAM. They said I was an eight-year-old prodigy so Mum said to just keep my mouth shut.

MACK. Ten years old and over the hill.

LAURA. / Oh my God.

TIMP. You're a twenty-one-year-old virgin?

CAM. Just fuck off!

MACK. The future's too busy making sure it's not past it to be doing very much else. Cam's investing in anti-wrinkle cream, not in fucking revolutions, mate.

BENNY. Why can't you try? What's so scary about it, Mack? Why does it – hurt you to try?

MACK. It's you that's going to hurt, Ben. Don't you see –
we're fucked. How well you do doesn't have anything to do
with how good you are – it's decided by some useless prick
somewhere acting out of fear or jealousy or greed – even if
you do alright, you're never going to earn what your parents
did, you're never going to be able to afford the house that
you grew up in – trying – all that nonsense out there –
wouldn't bother.

BENNY. If you try hard and you've got passion and you've got
fucking drive –

MACK. That what your mum said? What else is she going say –
eh? 'It's largely to do with timing, image and nepotism – so
always try and be in the right place at the right time, suck as
much cock as you can and find a way to be better looking
than God intended you'?

BENNY. I won't let you get in my head like you got in his.

MACK. I didn't get in anyone's head.

BENNY. You sure?

MACK. People make their own decisions.

Beat.

TIMP *picks up* LAURA *and spins her round.* TIMP *pours a
shot and offers it to* LAURA *– he sprinkles it with coke – as
if it's a magic potion.*

TIMP. It'll be magic.

LAURA. Yeah?

TIMP *nods.*

SOPHIE *corners* MACK *before he's able to leave to help*
CAM *with the rubbish.*

SOPHIE. Looks like we're here until morning.

MACK. Looks like it.

BENNY. Cam – no – we can't have any more.

SOPHIE. Wonder how long you'll last?

MACK. Think you should have a sit down, Sophs.

SOPHIE. It would be brilliant, we would be /

MACK. Cool off, calm down.

SOPHIE. Do you remember the colour of the sky?

BENNY. Stop it – Cam, stop bringing it in.

MACK (*turning from* SOPHIE). Leave him.

TIMP. I love you.

LAURA. I know.

BENNY. Stop bringing it in.

CAM. We have to.

BENNY. I said stop.

CAM. They told us to.

TIMP. Shall we have some fun?

LAURA. Course.

> LAURA *knocks back her first shot and hands the shot glass back to* TIMP.

More please.

SOPHIE (*getting louder*). Do you remember the colour of the sky?

> SOPHIE *gets up onto the table and starts dancing.*

> MACK *starts bringing the rubbish in with* CAM – BENNY *stands.*

BENNY. Stop. Stop.

> TIMP *refills the glass and goes to knock it back.* LAURA *stops him.*

LAURA. Na-uh. It's mine.

> LAURA *takes the shot glass from* TIMP *and sinks it herself.*

And again – let's go.

TIMP. You sure.

LAURA. Barely started, babe.

TIMP. Good on ya.

LAURA. More please. More please, Timp.

TIMP. Everything alright, babe?

LAURA. I said more please.

TIMP. Your wish is my command.

> TIMP *fills another shot.*

> It's party time.

LAURA. Damn right it fucking is.

> LAURA *sinks another shot.*

> MACK *and* CAM *keep bringing in the bags.*

BENNY. Stop it – fucking stop it.

SOPHIE. Mack – I don't feel bad. Mack?

> MACK *stops bringing the rubbish in and turns to her.*

BENNY. We didn't make this mess; this isn't our mess.

CAM. We have to /

BENNY. Stop bringing it in.

CAM. He said – we have to –

BENNY (*up close to* CAM). I said stop fucking bringing it in –
you hear me?

LAURA. You got any pills left?

TIMP. How many you taken already?

LAURA. None.

TIMP. That's not true, babe.

CAM. But they're police, Benny – we have to /

BENNY. Stop being such a fucking coward.

> CAM *stands opposite* BENNY *and juts his chin out.*

Now take these bags and put them back out there, because I've had enough – you hear? I've had enough of just bending over and taking it – I won't sink – I won't fucking sink – you hear? Pick 'em up.

CAM *stares at* BENNY.

SOPHIE. I don't feel bad.

MACK. Get down.

SOPHIE. I think it's worth it.

LAURA. Where are they? They in your pockets, babe? Are they?

LAURA *starts frisking* TIMP – TIMP *progressively uncomfortable tries to fend her off*.

TIMP. I think you've had enough.

BENNY. I said – Pick. Them. Up.

LAURA. Do you? I thought it was party time?

BENNY. Did you hear me?

MACK. Get down.

SOPHIE. Why won't you try, Mack?

LAURA *discovers* TIMP*'s pills on him – she pulls the bag out of his pocket*.

LAURA. Ah-ha!

SOPHIE. Why won't you try?

CAM*'s bottom lip starts to go.*

BENNY. Don't start fucking blubbing.

SOPHIE. For me?

TIMP. Give it here.

MACK *stares at* SOPHIE, *unable to move – unable to answer*.

LAURA. What's the problem – worried you won't have any left?

BENNY. I said pick up the fucking bags – Cam I – said – pick them the fuck up!

TIMP. Give it to me.

CAM, *sniffling, starts scrabbling around trying to pick up all the bags* – CAM *stands and sees out the window past* BENNY.

CAM. There's fire – look – they've, they've set fire to it – the city's on fire.

LAURA. You reckon there's enough in here to kill me?

LAURA *pops one in her mouth.*

BENNY *goes to look out of the window – dumbstruck – distraught.*

BENNY. Whole fucking lot's going to burn.

SOPHIE (*to* MACK). Do you remember the colour of the sky?

TIMP. Give me the bag.

TIMP *lunges at* LAURA *and grabs the bag off her.*

BENNY. Whole fucking lot's going to burn.

SOPHIE. Do you remember the colour of the sky?

MACK. Get down, Sophs. Please.

SOPHIE. Do you?

LAURA *opens her palm and reveals three pills.*

BENNY. Whole fucking lot's going to burn!

SOPHIE *starts to sing 'Ain't Got No/I Got Life' – loud on the table staring directly at* MACK, *he can't seem to move – to speak.*

LAURA *laughs.*

TIMP. Don't – don't do that. Please – don't, you'll hurt yourself.

LAURA *sinks the three pills and laughs.*

BENNY (*snaps – something has broken in him, he can't contain it any longer, he roars*). We're going to fucking burn and you're still not looking! If this is a party, where are all the people? Used to be hundreds showed up!

LAURA. What do you care – as long as I keep laughing?

BENNY. You're just fucking swallowing it and it's going explode inside you.

LAURA *laughs hard and throws a bin bag at* TIMP. TIMP *stumbles backwards into the rubbish.* CAM *and* MACK *start throwing bags as well. A huge rubbish fight starts – bags being lobbed, as if to throw the bags at each other is all that they can do. The fight gets harder and harder – more and more painful – they are hurting each other, the pace builds and builds and builds until they are exhausted – they pant, and stare – as if they have been tickled so hard it hurts.*

They stand – all of them breathless, barely able to get air into their lungs. Red-faced – half-laughing, half-crying – an exhausted silence falls.

Long pause.

It's still here.

SOPHIE *stares at* MACK.

SOPHIE. Are you crying?

MACK *wipes his face and walks slowly over to* BENNY, *he's choked, he comes in close to* BENNY, *he's shaking.*

MACK. Please be quiet, Benny.

BENNY *grabs* MACK, *it's forceful – it's the strongest we've seen him, there's real power and control in it –* BENNY *drags* MACK *to the untouched chair and forces him to look at it – we see* MACK *stare.* MACK *turns to* BENNY *– and looks at him, it seems amazingly tender – as if everything in him wants to give him a hug but he can't.*

BENNY. Look at it.

MACK *can't.*

MACK (*almost sobbing, pleading*). Please don't make me cut your tongue out.

BENNY. Say his name.

The boys stand and stare at one another – an eternity seems to pass between them, neither can move.

LAURA *stumbles to her feet.*

LAURA. Boys don't have tongues. They go silent when you come in the room. They don't say anything. It feels like they don't like you – like you're not friends at all. (*Silence.*) How many people has he fucked since I've been with him?

Long pause.

TIMP. I'm so glad you're standing up, babe.

LAURA. How many?

Pause.

BENNY. Ten, approximately ten, Loz.

LAURA. Thank you.

BENNY (*turning on* MACK). Say his name.

TIMP. Please don't /

TIMP *approaches* LAURA.

LAURA *jerks away.*

LAURA. Don't.

BENNY (*calm, stronger now*). Say his name.

MACK *stands – starts to shake, almost broken.*

BENNY *picks up a sushi knife and holds it up at* MACK.

I said – say his name.

Beat.

MACK. You want to believe someone will catch you whatever happens, but they won't. We aren't made to be able to stomach the real weakness of each other.

BENNY. Say it happened – say we let it happen.

BENNY *steps closer to* MACK.

MACK. Look at you – wide eyes and fucking needy and shrill and panicking – and asking, asking – fucking needing – it's repulsive. I find it – repulsive.

BENNY. Say his name.

MACK. I'm not your dad, Benny.

BENNY. Look me in the eye.

MACK. It's not my job to carry you.

BENNY. Fucking look at me – look at me, Mack.

MACK *keeps his eyes on the floor.*

You're my best mate. You're my best mate in the whole world.

MACK. We're on our own.

BENNY. Say his fucking name.

MACK. It's not our fault!

BENNY. Try!

MACK. He didn't – did he? He didn't fucking try at all. He just bailed out and left the mess for the rest of us to try and fucking clear up, expected us to get up in the fucking morning!

BENNY *lunges at* MACK *with the knife.*

MACK *swerves it.*

BENNY *stumbles forward bringing the knife swooping down towards the table.*

CAM *lunges forward and puts his hand beneath the blade – the tip of two fingers on his right hand are sliced off.*

MACK *grabs* CAM*'s hand and manically tries to stem the flow.*

No – fucking no.

BENNY *stands and stares.*

CAM (*smiling*). It was an accident.

Scene Four

The kitchen is empty except for TIMP, *who makes himself a cup of tea.*

The soft twilight of the early hours swims across the kitchen.

It is the first time we have seen him quiet, calm, alone.

TIMP, *on his own, is somehow a different creature entirely.*

TIMP *finds the cupcake and candle that* LAURA *had previously tried to give him.*

TIMP *sits with his tea, putting the cupcake in front of him and he stares at it.*

LAURA *enters; she's got a bag of stuff with her.*

LAURA*'s still high – she's gurning and can't focus very easily.*

Pause.

TIMP. Twentieth birthday – my dad gave me a hip flask – and I had to work, at the restaurant – I was new, floor staff – that night, even though it was my birthday, so I filled up that flask and I went in to work with it. And it's really fucking funny, right – I'd had a bit to drink and I'd go and pick up the plates from the service hatch, and I'd stop in the corridor so I could see the faces of the fat rich fucks, all angry and waiting for their food and I'd just stand. I'd just stop and watch 'em waiting for me – getting angrier and angrier – and I thought I'll just stand here cos it's my birthday and they can fucking wait a bit longer; never waited more than a few seconds each time – but I felt like a fucking king. Isn't that funny?

Beat.

I was angry having to work – cos before that my birthday was always in the summer holidays. It's mad, I've been working full time for ten years and I still always – every year – expect there to be a summer holiday. Never is though. (*Beat.*) You still fucked?

LAURA. I've been sick. It's helped.

TIMP. Good.

TIMP *goes to touch* LAURA, *she steps away from him.*

Beat.

Sort of can't fucking believe I'll never get another summer holiday.

LAURA. I know.

LAURA *stands.*

TIMP. Thought we could go on a trip – just you and /

LAURA. Haven't got any leave left cos of helping Mum move house.

TIMP. Right. You want water or tea or – a – any /

LAURA. I'm going to go, Timp.

TIMP. You don't want to be alone in that state.

LAURA *takes a step towards the door.*

You coming back?

Beat.

I never thought I'd be lucky enough to land you.

LAURA *turns to go.*

It's not because I don't l[ove] – it's – it's not even the – it's just – just the window to put the party in – it's so small, you got to make the party really big.

LAURA. Doesn't feel like a party.

Beat.

TIMP. No.

TIMP *moves towards* LAURA *to hold her.*

LAURA. Can't though – undo things. (*Beat.*) Funny you being thirty.

Pause.

TIMP. Not that funny.

LAURA. No.

LAURA *goes to leave.*

TIMP. Loz?

LAURA. Yeah

Long pause – TIMP *thinks – he's got nothing.*

Where you going to live when the boys leave?

Beat.

TIMP. Couple of the freshers from the party the other night said they might move in – fill the spots. I might stay on.

Beat.

LAURA. Right.

Beat.

LAURA *leaves*

TIMP *sits back down in front of the candle and lights it – he watches it burn.*

BENNY *enters.*

TIMP *stares at him.*

BENNY *goes over to the window and looks out.*

BENNY. They've put most of it out.

TIMP. Yeah?

BENNY. Is Laura still /

TIMP. No – she's gone.

BENNY. She'll be fucking dancing till tomorrow night.

BENNY *tries to laugh a little,* TIMP *won't go with him.*

TIMP. She was sick.

BENNY. Right. (*Beat.*) I'm sorry, Timp – I'm really sorry – I shouldn't have, I didn't have a right to.

TIMP. Course you did; you're her mate.

Pause.

BENNY. Is it your birthday?

TIMP. Yeah; fucking thirty.

BENNY. No?

TIMP. Yeah.

Beat.

BENNY. Timp – what's your name?

TIMP. What?

BENNY. On the contract this morning it said C. Timpson and I
realised I don't know your first name.

Pause.

TIMP. It's Colin.

Beat.

They both laugh – it is a relief.

BENNY. Oh.

TIMP. Yeah – alright.

BENNY. I'd stick with Timp, mate.

TIMP. Thanks.

Silence falls.

You seen any more pills about?

Beat.

BENNY *nods, picks one up off the table.*

Alright if I have it?

BENNY. Course.

BENNY *hands the pill to* TIMP.

TIMP *takes it.*

TIMP. Ta.

BENNY *nods.*

Benny?

BENNY. Yeah.

TIMP. Will you come and watch some Disney with me – for a bit? Just till I'm –

BENNY. Course… Colin.

The boys go to leave – before they do, SOPHIE *enters, she's carrying a bag.*

Sophs.

SOPHIE. Hi.

TIMP. We're going to watch a Disney movie, you game?

SOPHIE. Plane leaves in a few hours. I'll see ya.

TIMP. See ya.

TIMP exits.

BENNY. Bye, Sophs.

SOPHIE *hugs* BENNY *goodbye.*

SOPHIE. Benny, I /

BENNY. I'm going to go watch some Disney.

BENNY *leaves.*

SOPHIE *stands, surveys the room.*

SOPHIE *stands on Peter's chair.*

SOPHIE. I'm sorry, Peter.

MACK *enters.*

MACK *sees her standing on the chair and stops in his tracks.*

MACK. What you doing?

SOPHIE. Wondered what it looked like from up here.

MACK. And?

SOPHIE. Smaller.

MACK *nods.*

MACK *helps her down – it's gallant.*

MACK. You want /

SOPHIE (*laughing softly*). Tea? No.

Pause.

SOPHIE *stares at* MACK.

MACK. What?

SOPHIE. Nothing.

MACK. What you looking at?

SOPHIE *shrugs.*

It's like I'm a fucking hero. Like you're expecting me to fucking levitate or something.

SOPHIE *looks away, hurt.*

No one ever looks at me like that.

SOPHIE. Like it?

MACK. Feels like you're asking for something, for something I don't have. (*Pause.*) You got so much – of this... even when you're being a fucking mentalist – you got like... grace – somehow.

SOPHIE. No I /

MACK. I'm just a person. Pretty shit one at that.

SOPHIE. No you're not.

MACK. It can't be fucking dawn for ever, Sophs.

SOPHIE. I know. But it could be /

MACK. What?

SOPHIE. We could go away.

MACK. There's not a fucking country we can fly to where he's still alive – where we can talk him through it, where it hasn't happened how it has.

SOPHIE. I know.

MACK. Do you? Do you really?

SOPHIE. Yes.

MACK. We can't fly back to that fucking evening and just /

MACK stops himself – he looks at her in the twilight.

You are the most beautiful thing I think I've ever fucking seen.

Beat.

SOPHIE. Will you do your seagull impression?

MACK. What?

SOPHIE. Will you? Please.

MACK. No.

SOPHIE. Please.

MACK. Fuck off.

SOPHIE. Quietly.

MACK does his seagull impression.

He stops and looks at her.

She smiles.

I don't think you're a god. You're not even a very good seagull.

MACK. Thanks.

Beat – they smile.

SOPHIE. Come with me. Just see.

MACK. Then what?

SOPHIE. Don't know.

MACK. Come back, tell Benny – make even more fucking mess.

SOPHIE. Maybe it will be worth it.

MACK. I can't... when I, when I – look at you – it's like, in my head, you're always crying.

SOPHIE. I'll stop. Eventually.

MACK. Ever since – it's amazing how something like that – um – how it, sorry. It – it starts ripping the walls down – you know? It's like that morning – since then everything just emptied – like words are lies before they've even got out your mouth.

SOPHIE *kisses* MACK *tenderly. She holds his face.*

SOPHIE *steps back.*

SOPHIE. My plane leaves in two hours.

MACK. Where you going?

SOPHIE. Italy.

MACK. Oh, *bonjour*.

SOPHIE. That's France.

MACK. Oh yeah.

Pause.

I can't.

SOPHIE. Please.

MACK. No.

SOPHIE. I don't want it to start hurting, yet.

MACK. I'm sorry.

SOPHIE. Okay.

SOPHIE *grits her teeth and leaves.*

MACK *watches her go.*

MACK *hears the door slam – stands a moment and exits.*

ACT THREE

Scene One

The sun is up – it is a bright morning, sunlight streaks in through the windows.

BENNY *enters in his dressing gown.*

BENNY *goes to his brother's cupboard and takes out a packet of Coco Pops. He pours himself a bowl of Coco Pops and fills it with milk.*

BENNY *stands wondering where the hell he is going to find a spoon in the mess.*

TIMP *enters, he's in his pants – Mohican organised, chipper and bubbly.*

TIMP. Alright, Benny-boy – you seen my whites? I'm late as fuck and I can't find 'em anywhere.

BENNY. You going to work?

TIMP. Yeah. Only gone and fixed that fucking window the fuckers.

BENNY. Bloody hell.

TIMP. I'd take it off but two black marks already – can't risk it.

BENNY. Aren't you fucked?

TIMP. You got any fucking idea how boring that job is if you're not? You couldn't have a look out there for me – whilst I scout in here, could ya?

BENNY. Will you look for a spoon?

TIMP. What?

BENNY. I can't find a spoon for me Coco Pops.

TIMP. Right. Hey, Benny?

BENNY. Yeah?

TIMP. I was thinking – I could do with a fucking party tonight – you know – few beers?

Pause. BENNY *looks at* TIMP.

BENNY. Alright if I have a little think about that?

TIMP. Course.

BENNY *exits.*

TIMP *searches through the rubbish, trying to find his clothes.*

TIMP *pulls out a hugely long novelty spoon from the rubbish.*

Hey, Ben! Look at this – it's that massive spoon from Frankenstein's! Ha!

TIMP *drops the spoon at the middle.*

Benny, come and have a look! Ew it's all sticky.

TIMP *sniffs it – winces.*

Euch – it's fucking sambuca – I think I'm going to /

LAURA *enters, she's dressed for work.*

TIMP *hears her enter but doesn't turn around.*

TIMP *turns, retching and holding the massive spoon.*

Oh, hello.

LAURA. Hello.

TIMP. Laura, I –

LAURA. That's a big spoon.

TIMP. Yes.

LAURA. Don't tell me you're looking for your whites?

TIMP. Laura.

LAURA. You're late you do know that – they'll cut your bollocks off, that's every day this week.

TIMP *looks at her.*

What?

Beat.

We need to go, come on.

TIMP. Course.

LAURA. Fucking state in here.

TIMP. Laura?

LAURA (*sees his whites underneath a chair*). They're here, you plonker. Hurry up, you dumb fuck.

TIMP *stalls – he's genuinely moved.*

What? Why you staring? Will you hurry the fuck up?

LAURA *leaves.*

TIMP *jumps into his whites.*

BENNY *enters.*

BENNY. I couldn't find them – Laura's in the –

TIMP *kisses* BENNY *full on the mouth.*

TIMP *spanks* BENNY *on the bum with the spoon.*

TIMP *exits.*

BENNY *picks up the spoon and also discovers it's sticky in the middle.*

BENNY *goes to wash the spoon but the sink is full.*

BENNY *gives up and holds the spoon at the far end.*

BENNY *tries to eat the Coco Pops with the spoon but it is slightly longer than he can maneuver into his mouth.*

BENNY *tries again and the Coco Pops spill.*

MACK *enters – he has a large bag slung across his body, he's dressed to leave.*

BENNY *looks at him.*

Beat.

MACK. What's that?

BENNY. Coco Pops.

MACK. Why you eating it like a retard?

BENNY. Can't find any fucking cutlery.

MACK. What's that?

BENNY. Monster spoon, from Frankenstein's. Remember?
Meant to be like Frankenstein's spoon.

MACK. Hold it lower down.

BENNY. It's sticky in the middle with Sambuca.

MACK. Wash it.

BENNY. Sink's full.

Pause.

MACK. Come here.

MACK *goes to feed* BENNY *his Coco Pops.*

BENNY. No you're alright – no – come on –

MACK. Open your mouth.

BENNY. Fuck off.

MACK. Open your fucking mouth.

It looks like MACK *is going to feed* BENNY *from the spoon
– when he picks up the bowl instead.*

BENNY (*with his mouth open*). Don't fucking throw it at me.

MACK. Just drink it from the bowl. You dumb ass.

BENNY. Right.

MACK. Don't need a spoon.

BENNY. Yeah. Long night, eh?

MACK. Not long enough to be that retarded.

Beat.

BENNY. What's the bag for?

MACK. I'm going.

BENNY. Right.

MACK. I've left enough cash for…

Beat.

You heard from Cam?

BENNY. No.

MACK. Will you tell him – I'd stick about but / (*Checks his watch.*)

BENNY. Yeah.

MACK. Thanks.

Beat.

BENNY. He was selfish. You're right. Cop-out – left us to clear it up – eh? Just us. Not very good at it.

MACK. No.

BENNY. I – I – miss you. I'm sorry if that sounds /

MACK. I've really got to go.

BENNY. Alright.

MACK. Ben – ?

BENNY. Yeah.

MACK. I think it will – get better – eventually.

Pause.

MACK *turns to go.*

Beat.

BENNY. Better have me Coco Pops back then.

MACK. Sorry.

MACK *goes to hand* BENNY *the bowl of Coco Pops.*

Oh hello.

MACK *spots something, a little toy soldier floating in the bowl.*

You got the prize. Little soldier. Bang. There you go.

BENNY. You have it.

Beat.

MACK. Thanks.

BENNY. Fingers crossed.

BENNY *goes to hug* MACK.

MACK *offers him his hand.*

BENNY *nods and shakes it.*

MACK *exits.*

BENNY *cries.*

Scene Two

The door opens – BENNY *thinks it's* MACK.

BENNY. Thank fuck for /

CAM *enters.*

Oh – Cam.

BENNY *recovers himself.*

Mate, you're back. What happened?

CAM. Where's Mack off to?

BENNY. Holiday.

CAM. What?

BENNY. I think. How's the hand?

CAM. Bit sore.

BENNY. What were the nurses like?

CAM. Wouldn't stop rolling her eyes and saying it was amazing how little pain I was feeling considering the injury.

BENNY. What's it like out there?

CAM. Mad. Trees all look like little burnt matchsticks – shite everywhere. Funny though – once you're out at the Western General, out the city – you can see the hills in the distance all clean and green and – it's like nothing ever went wrong, feel silly for thinking… then you drive back in and it's like it'll never get clean. You sort of can't work out how much to – how worried to /

BENNY. Yeah.

BENNY *smiles at him.*

BENNY *goes to the window to look out.*

You want tea?

CAM. Yes please. Can you put a bit of sugar in it?

BENNY. Course. Funny how the first bit of morning always looks a bit like a sunset. You reckon you could tell – if someone just woke you up and said – dawn or dusk – you reckon you could tell?

CAM. Rises in the east, sets in the west.

BENNY. Not this far north. Up and down in almost the same spot.

Beat.

CAM. It's fucked – right through Cowgate – all the old town; fire started down at the Parliament and just went right on up.

BENNY. That's all the library stores; burnt their own fucking books, the idiots.

CAM. Didn't even fucking touch the Parliament Building – you know what I mean? What is that – all that old stuff, all cobbles and history and fucking thousands of years of – and it burns in just one night because of some fucking… and that fucking ugly son of a bitch Parliament Building is still standing. Blows your mind.

BENNY *hands* CAM *his tea – he goes to take it with his right hand – but realises it's bandaged and has to take it with his left.*

BENNY. You sad about it?

CAM. The fire?

BENNY. Your hand.

CAM. I –

BENNY. I can't even say how sorry I – I mean for ever I'll – did they say there were ways of fixing it, of /

CAM. Shut up, man. I'm glad.

BENNY. What do you mean you're glad?

CAM. It was the weirdest thing, she's sitting there telling me I'll never play again, not like I had before and I felt so much – better. I'm not sure I even really wanted to do it, I never chose to – I was just good at it and so that was it – and it seemed stupid not doing something that you were good at but – I never wanted to.

BENNY. You don't mean that.

CAM. It's fucking great – I feel fucking great. I can do what I want now and I didn't even have to make the decision.

BENNY. What do you want to do?

CAM. Don't know yet.

BENNY. Right.

CAM. Think I might apply to university.

BENNY *laughs.*

It'll be four years before I'm out – so maybe – things will have… you know…

BENNY. Good idea, pal. You want a biscuit?

CAM. Yes please.

BENNY *finds one and gives it to him.*

BENNY. Last summer – me and Pete – we ended up in this
    cathedral together – it was a family holiday, Mum and Dad
    were having an argument outside so he and I decided to go
    in. It was all dark, except these little red candles; you know
    those racks of candles, in lines, where you're meant to pay
    and you light it and it's for someone in heaven? They had
    one of them, but it was modern – so the candles were little
    LED thingies, you know electric. And this woman comes up,
    Spanish, big fat one, red lips, black hair – and she puts the
    euro in the slot and one of the candles flickers a bit, but it
    goes out. It doesn't work, right? So she waddles over to
    complain. This electrician comes over and he's really
    sweating and he unlocks the back of this thing and you can
    see all the wires. She sees all the wires, right? The electrician
    fiddles with it finishes and locks the thing back down and
    gives her back her euro. The old woman puts her money in
    the slot… and one candle lights up… and she prays, she
    prays like she really fucking means it.

    Beat.

CAM. This another God squad thing, Ben?

BENNY. Even though she'd seen the wiring.

CAM. So?

BENNY. I said it was fucking idiotic. Made me angry. Turned to
    Peter – he were crying. It was the last time I saw him cry – he
    said it was fucking amazing, being able to do what she did.

    Beat.

CAM. Don't get it.

BENNY. Never mind.

    The pair of them look at the room.

    We should get his lot tidied up.

CAM. In a bit.

BENNY. You want to give me a hand?

CAM. What you going to do with it.

BENNY. Don't know, yet.

The buzzer goes.

Who's that?

CAM. I'll get it.

CAM *exits.*

BENNY *looks at the rubbish.*

BENNY *finds a bin bag – heads over to his brother's cupboard and starts to empty it into the bin bag. Job complete, he turns back to the kitchen and looks at the mess – he's overwhelmed.*

CAM *enters – he's carrying a jumper.*

BENNY. And?

CAM. It was the Renault Mégane.

BENNY. What did she want?

CAM. Said to give this back to Mack – said to thank him – for stopping her.

BENNY *goes over and takes the jumper from* CAM.

BENNY. I gave him this.

The jumper has He-Man on it.

CAM. Will we put some music on – help us tidy?

BENNY. iPod got fucked. Stereo still works though.

CAM *turns it on and the tuner fuzzes.*

CAM *looks out at the room.*

CAM. You reckon we'll get this tidied up?

BENNY. Yeah.

CAM. You think or you know?

BENNY. I think.

CAM *switches it to CD and presses play.*

BENNY *looks at the jumper and puts it on.*

A violin solo plays – beautiful, haunting.

What's this?

Beat.

CAM. It's me.

Beat.

BENNY *tries to tidy again but gives up quickly.*

CAM *stares out into the morning… listening – realising.*

BENNY *picks up his Coco Pops bowl and drinks from the bowl – chocolate milk spills down the front of the He-Man jumper – he tries to clean it off.*

Pause.

Lights down.

End of play.

A Nick Hern Book

Boys first published in Great Britain as a paperback original in 2012 by
Nick Hern Books Limited, The Glasshouse, 49a Goldhawk Road, London
W12 8QP, in association with HighTide Festival Theatre, Headlong and
The Nuffield

Reprinted 2012

Boys copyright © 2012 Ella Hickson

Ella Hickson has asserted her right to be identified as the author of this
work

Cover image by Léo-Oaul Billès
Cover design by Ned Hoste, 2H

Typeset by Nick Hern Books, London
Printed in the UK by Mimeo Ltd, Huntingdon, Cambridgeshire PE29 6XX

A CIP catalogue record for this book is available from the British Library

ISBN   978 1 84842 262 9